Great Cake
DECORATING

SWEET DESIGNS *for* CAKES & CUPCAKES

Great Cake
DECORATING

Erin Gardner

The Taunton Press

The Taunton Press, Inc., 63 South Main Street, PO Box 5506,
Newtown, CT 06470-5506
e-mail: tp@taunton.com

Editor: Renee Iwaszkiewicz Neiger
Copy editor: Nina Rynd Whitnah
Indexer: Heidi Blough
Jacket/Cover design: Kimberly Adis
Interior design: Kimberly Adis
Layout: Kimberly Adis
Illustrator: Andrew Wanke, except for p. ii by Laura Condouris
Photo editor: Erin Giunta
Photographer: Mark Davidson
Photoshoot location: The Rivermill
Prop stylist: Rowena Day
Author photographer: Mark Corliss Photography

The following names/manufacturers appearing in *Great Cake Decorating* are trademarks: Ateco®, Cake Central®, Ferrero Rocher®, Fondarific®, Lyle's Golden Syrup®, Masonite®, Necco® wafers, Satin Ice®, Smarties®, Styrofoam™, X-ACTO®

Library of Congress Cataloging-in-Publication Data

Gardner, Erin.
 Great cake decorating : sweet designs for cakes & cupcakes / Erin Gardner.
    pages cm
   ISBN 978-1-62113-760-3 (pbk.)
1. Cake decorating. 2. Icings (Confectionery) I. Title.
 TX771.2.G34 2014
 641.86'539--dc23
                        2013038862

For Maxwell

Acknowledgments

Thanks to the following: Mike, my wonderful husband and best friend (who will most likely be made a saint for this whole experience), for being by my side throughout my entire crazy career and eagerly supporting every wild idea.

My sister, Kelly, for making fondant horses, decorating cakes when I had a broken arm, and so much more. You're always there for me and words can't express just what your support means to me.

My parents, for their amazing support and business advice, and for being terrific grandparents.

Kayla, for your organization, hard work, and humor; for going above and beyond the role of baker, allowing me to even think about taking on a project like this one.

Jaime Avalos Chichizola, for being a friend when I needed one most. Thank you for being so generous with your knowledge and experience, and for pushing me in the right direction.

Renee Neiger, my fabulous editor, for bringing this project into my life and helping me realize one of my dreams. Your guidance and encouragement have been invaluable. I will forever be indebted to that sombrero-wearing cupcake!

To the staff at Taunton Press, including Erin Giunta, for your sharp eye and attention to detail, Kim Adis, for your creativity and excitement while designing this book, and Amy Griffin, for making it all fit.

Mark Davidson, my friend and the photographer who so beautifully captured all of the images in this book, for being so dedicated to this project and for always making my cakes look so pretty. Thank you to the Rivermill, rivermillnh.com, for hosting the photoshoot and Be Our Guest, beourguestpartyrental.com, for their beautiful china and linens. And to my cousin, Shelley Barandes, of Albertine Press for the gorgeous paper goods and antique letterpress blocks.

Mrs. Burns, for telling me I was an artist.

My clients, for trusting me to create cakes for their important life events, constantly inspiring me, and challenging me to create new things.

To my wonderful friends; huge, amazing family; and the talented vendors I get to work with every day. I'm so blessed to be surrounded by such encouraging, inspiring, and supportive people.

Contents

Introduction

"Great cake decorating doesn't have to be complicated or difficult. It just takes planning, practice, and patience."

I LOVE CAKE DECORATING, BUT IT WASN'T ALWAYS SO. WHEN STARTING MY sweets career in the fast-paced restaurant world, I didn't think I had the time for custom cake creations. I dreaded creating cakes for special occasions.

I overcame my fear by starting with the basics—I put together simple buttercream cakes per clients' requests. Then, I gave fondant a try. I soon realized that working with it combined my love of desserts with my more artistic skills like sculpting, painting, and drawing, and began to enjoy creating custom cakes.

It was during this time that I received an email about a gum paste flower class to be taught by famed sugar artist Ron Ben Israel; the email included pictures of his cakes and sugar flowers. I wondered how it was possible to create something so realistic, so beautiful. I took the class, and it changed me. I thought "Why not make cakes full time?"

Throughout the years I learned that great cake decorating doesn't have to be complicated or difficult. It just takes planning, practice, and patience. Think about what you want to create before doing it, and then figure out the best way to get there. When the plan changes (which it is sometimes bound to do), be flexible and work around it. The biggest secret to great cake decorating is to learn the basic techniques and then practice them. As with anything, building a solid foundation of techniques allows you to then layer and combine them in exciting new ways—the possibilities are endless.

I know how valuable your time is, which is why I've tried to share designs that will get you the biggest return on your investment. I've shared some of my basic decorating techniques along with helpful "Make It or Fake It" tips. These tips offer shortcuts for time-pressed decorators—you can probably find some great cake decorating ideas right in your pantry.

Designing cakes is my favorite part of the job. I love to think about the people the cake is for and their interests and favorite things. I also love to take classic designs and techniques and use them in new ways. Don't be afraid to make the ideas in this book your own by changing colors and shapes and playing with scale.

Having a cake that tastes as good as it looks has always been very important to me, which is why I've also shared a few of my favorite recipes for cakes, fillings, and frostings. Whether you're baking multiple tiers for a large special event, single servings for a bake sale, or a small cake for an intimate gathering, the recipes and design variations I've included cater to every serving size.

As you get started, it's important to remember that cake decorating shouldn't be stressful. Accidents happen. Breakage happens. We're only human, and well—it's cake. Even the most seasoned cake decorators can get down on themselves from time to time. If the worst happens, try to stay calm and use what you have to make the best of it. Most of the time we're making cakes for other people, and it's that thoughtfulness and use of your time that are really most important. That's why no matter what, always remember: Your cake is awesome!

PART ONE

Make It Pretty

Make Cake

I KNOW YOU WANT TO GET RIGHT TO DECORATING, BUT A GREAT cake is as good as it looks *and tastes*. As a pastry chef, I learned that the first secret to great cake decorating is having the perfect base on which to build! Great cakes start from the inside out. To get the correct foundation, you need to know some cake-baking basics. Too often, people sabotage their cake making by using the wrong tools or rushing through steps; the result can be a cake that's too dark and dry or one with edges that are too crusty.

So let's start by going over the basics. I've shared it all. From baking to leveling to stacking to crumb-coating, here are some cake-making tools and tips to ensure that you start off with a perfect cake.

Better Baking Tools

CHOOSING THE RIGHT CAKE PAN SEEMS LIKE AN EASY ENOUGH TASK, RIGHT? But because there are so many to choose from, knowing what to look for helps. Where to begin? First, figure out the cake (or cakes) you want to make, and then pick the tools you need. Here are a few of my must-haves and nice-to-haves.

Rounds

Round pans are the most versatile, since round cakes are the easiest to fill and cover. Always buy pans with straight edges. Some have slightly tapered sides, which make it difficult to stack and fill a cake. Also, look for light-colored pans, because darker pans will give cakes a darker, tougher crust.

I bake in even-numbered size rounds (6 inch, 8 inch, 10 inch, etc.), but cake pans come in odd-numbered sizes as well. Professionally, I find it easier to use either all even-numbered or all odd-numbered; it depends on which will stack best for the design and from a serving perspective. At home, use whichever size pans work best for you.

Shapes

Besides round pans, a good set of square pans is useful. Invest in those before moving on to any other pan shape. Pans come in all sorts of shapes and sizes now. Some popular ones include hexagons, ovals, and hearts.

Half-sheet pans (or cookie sheets)

What you call a cookie sheet, we in commercial baking call a half-sheet pan. These pans work well for baking thin sheets of cake that can be used to create mini cakes. The most useful one to have has smooth rounded edges on all sides and a light-colored surface. As with cake pans, the darker the color of the pan, the darker and tougher the crust on your cake (or cookies, for that matter) will be.

Sheet cake pans

Sheet cake pans are deeper than the standard sheet pan. The most useful size is 11 inches × 15 inches. When buying a pan, look for one with straight sides and hard corners and edges. If you have a pan with rounded edges, you can trim the sides of the cake after it has cooled to create sharper corners. Since I don't make sheet cakes professionally, I use mine to cut mini cakes or to stack and carve shaped cakes.

Cupcake pans

These come in three basic sizes: mini, standard, and jumbo. Standard pans bake a dozen at once. Mini pans typically bake two dozen, and jumbo pans bake a half-dozen at a time. Cupcakes are great for cake decorating, because you can stack, trim, and flip them upside down to achieve many different shapes. Cupcake pans are also a great place to keep fondant or gum paste decorations when waiting for them to dry overnight.

Dome pans

These are half-circle cake pans. The larger forms come with a base to set the rounded pan into for baking. The smaller forms make six at a time, but unless you plan on making 50 baseball-shaped mini cakes, they're not necessary. A little secret: Stainless steel bowls do essentially the same thing. Make sure the bowl you want to use is stainless steel and oven-safe before you bake in it.

Cake rings and bundt pans

Bundt pans are terrific when baking cakes for brunches or holiday parties. Some are perfectly smooth and round, while others have beautifully shaped curves and ridges around the outer edge. A smooth, light-colored pan will be more versatile for decorating purposes. The more detailed pans are perfect to use when you have little time for decorating but still need a pretty cake.

Cake forms

Teddy bears, ducks, guitars, and more—these forms can be so tempting to buy, but I actually find them very limiting. Most shapes can be created by combining and trimming circles and squares. And while they seem like a time-saver, they can actually end up causing more of a headache in the end by limiting the kind of cake, filling, and finish that you can use.

Stainless steel bowls

Most kitchen bowls are plastic, ceramic, or metal. For most uses (mixing batters, tinting frostings, etc.) any kind will do. My preference is to have a good set of stainless steel bowls in assorted sizes and one plastic bowl for use in the microwave. Stainless ends up being the most versatile, because you can bake in them and use them over water baths. A microwave-safe plastic bowl comes in handy for melting small quantities of chocolate, candy melts, and butter in the microwave.

Parchment paper

This paper is perfect for lining cake pans. The rolls sold at the supermarket can be difficult to use, because the paper is curled. I prefer parchment paper that comes in full and half-sheet pan sizes. It can be tough to find in some supermarkets but is easily found online.

Cupcake cups

Greaseproof paper baking cups are the best kind to bake in, and they come in a variety of colors and patterns. Silicone baking cups also work well and are great for baking at home since they are reusable. When baking with silicone cups, you should still place them in a cupcake pan or on a cookie sheet so that they are easier to handle.

MEASURING TIPS

Accuracy in baking is important, so here are a few helpful measuring tips:

- **USE THE RIGHT TOOL FOR THE JOB.** There is a difference between wet and dry measuring cups and using the wrong one will affect the outcome of your recipe. Steer clear of cute cups shaped like nesting dolls or hearts, because it's hard to be confident in their accuracy.

- **WHEN MEASURING FLOUR, DO NOT USE YOUR MEASURING CUP AS A SCOOP.** Rather, scoop the flour into the cup with a spoon until it loosely piles up over the top of the cup. Level the top of the cup with the back of a knife. Cocoa powder should be measured the same way.

- **FIRMLY PACK BROWN SUGAR INTO THE MEASURING CUP.** Press the brown sugar into the cup until it is level with the top of the cup.

- **USE THE MEASURING TOOL CALLED FOR IN THE RECIPE.** Not all weights and measures are interchangeable. For example, an 8-ounce cup of flour actually weighs about 5 ounces.

- **PROPERLY MEASURE TEASPOONS AND TABLESPOONS.** Teaspoons and tablespoons should be filled and leveled. Use spoons made for baking, not the ones in your silverware drawer.

Cake-Making Tools

THESE ARE THE TOOLS I USE ON EVERY CAKE, AND I REFER TO THEM FREQUENTLY throughout the book. They are great for creating basic cakes—the canvas on which all of your designs will be made.

1. Long serrated knife

You'll need a good-quality serrated knife for leveling and splitting cakes. My serrated knife is 18 inches long with a 12-inch blade. Wielding this kind of knife can be scary at first, but once you're used to it, you'll feel like a one tough caker! When using any knife, focus on the task at hand, and always be aware of the placement of your hand and fingers.

2. Cake drums or bases

Cake drums are thick cardboard bases covered in colored foil on which the finished cake sits. They can be found at any store that sells cake and craft supplies. For heavier cakes, you can have a wooden round cut at a hardware store, or you can search cake decorating supply stores and web sites for precut wooden or Masonite® rounds.

3. Cake boards

These are thin, unfinished cardboard cake rounds that go in between tiers to add stability to a cake or under a cake that will be moved to a cake stand when completed.

4. Turntable

They can range from very inexpensive to more of an investment. The best turntables have strong, sturdy bases, like metal or cast iron, with a level, smooth-rolling top. My favorite turntable is the classic Ateco® 612 with the cast iron base. The less-expensive plastic turntables are okay, but they get gummed up pretty quickly. There is nothing worse than being in a piping groove and having the turntable and cake stop short while the piping bag keeps going. I can't overemphasize how much a good turntable will affect your cake decorating!

5. Metal ruler

I prefer metal because it holds its shape better than wood or plastic. A 12-inch ruler should work for most projects. If you plan to make larger cakes, you may want to pick up a yardstick or tape measure.

6. Metal spatulas

These are what you picture when you think of a cake decorator's spatula. They come with plastic or wooden handles. I prefer plastic handles for ease of cleaning and because the wooden handles tend to deteriorate more quickly due to frequent washing. I use metal spatulas in a variety of sizes for different techniques. Along with my rolling pin, my metal spatulas are my go-to tools. Everyone's hands are different, so you'll have to try a few different sizes to see what feels best for you. These are the sizes in my tool kit:

- Long straight blade (11-inch spatula, 6-inch blade)
- Long angled blade (13-inch spatula, 7¾-inch blade)
- Small straight blade (8-inch spatula, 4 inch blade)
- Small angled blade (9-inch spatula, 4½-inch blade)
- Small angled blade with tapered end (8-inch spatula, 4-inch blade)

7. Level

A level can be found in any hardware store and will help ensure that your cake has a flat top. I use a level that is about 6 inches long. It's easy to work with and fits nicely in a tool box.

8. X-ACTO® knife or scalpel

A very sharp, clean blade is helpful for cutting out shapes, trimming edges, and adding detail. Scalpels come in multipacks. They are less expensive than X-ACTO knives and work just as well; plus, they are disposable. If you prefer, you can use a small, sharp knife instead.

9. Fondant smoother

The best fondant smoothers are made from a solid piece of clear acrylic or heavy plastic. Avoid ones that have a seam in the middle, because it can pull on the fondant. Smoothers have either rounded or flat edges and are sold in sets of two. I like to use one of each kind, because I can get a sharper edge that way.

10. Scissors

I always keep two pairs of scissors in my kit. I use one for nonedible items like trimming cake boards, cutting small dowels, and cutting templates. The other I use when working with fondant. Scissors come in handy when trimming square edges or working with fabric techniques. Label the handles so you don't mix them up—nothing dulls scissors faster than cutting through paper.

11. Rubber spatulas

Flexible silicone spatulas are the best—the ones that are made in one solid piece. Spatulas that are made with the blade glued to the handle always seem to come apart, and I'm not all that confident in their ability to be cleaned. Always buy the heat-safe ones, because there's nothing worse than melted plastic in your caramel!

12. Dowels

You can use wooden or plastic dowels for stacking cakes. Cake decorating supply stores typically sell both in a variety of thicknesses.

13. Plastic rolling pins

When buying a rolling pin, it's okay to be picky. Find one that you really enjoy using, because it will be used often. Smooth plastic rolling pins create the best results when rolling fondant or gum paste, because they don't leave marks or absorb food color like wooden ones can. Have at least two sizes on hand: one large pin (about 14 inches) for rolling out fondant to cover cakes and a smaller one (4 to 6 inches) for working with gum paste or smaller shapes.

Piping Tools

THERE ARE SO MANY DIFFERENT SHAPES AND SIZES OF PIPING TIPS AVAILABLE THAT figuring out what's needed can be confusing. To help you decide which one to invest in first, learn what tip works best for each task.

1. Basketweave tips
This tip has a long, thin opening with one smooth and one ridged side. It's used most frequently to create basketweave patterns or flat ruffles.

2. Star tips
The pointed star-shaped opening on top can be used to pipe rosettes or shells.

3. Round tips
These come in a variety of sizes and are useful for writing and piping lines and dots.

4. Specialty tips
There really is a tip for everything! You'll find numerous variations on the tips listed here as well as tips that pipe hearts and even pine trees.

5. Leaf tips
This tip has a triangular shape to it, with thin open sides. It's useful for piping leaves, petals, and ruffles.

6. Couplers
Couplers allow you to change tips on your piping bags without using multiple bags. They are made from two pieces of plastic; one gets dropped inside the piping bag, and the other is screwed on from the outside.

7. Piping bags
Heavy plastic disposable piping bags work best. (I prefer not to use reusable piping bags because they are difficult to keep sanitary.) They are usually made from thicker plastic—sandwich bags, which are thinner, don't hold up well to lots of pressure when piping. In a pinch, a zip-top plastic freezer bag will do. Paper cones made from parchment paper are great for small piping projects, like writing a name on a cake, but stick to the plastic bags for larger projects like frosting cupcakes.

Splitting & Filling Cake

THE BEST DECORATING IDEA IN THE WORLD WILL BE LOST ON YOUR GUESTS IF THEY ARE distracted by a cake that is lopsided, lumpy, or bulging at the sides. The techniques in this section are the cake fundamentals. Take time to build a great base, and decorating will be so much easier. For simplicity's sake, the cakes in this book are baked in round or square pans, but the level-and-split method works for any cake shape.

Splitting Cake

Once the cake has cooled all the way through, you will need to level its domed top.

1. Apply a small smear of buttercream (about the size of a half dollar for a regular-sized cake, more for larger cakes) to a cake board that's the same diameter as the cake round. This ensures that the cake will stick when placed on the board.

2. Place the cake on the board. Turn the pan that the cake was baked in upside down, and place it near the baked cake. Use the pan as your guide and run a serrated knife across the top of the cake to cut it level.

3. Once the cake is leveled, use a metal ruler to find the center point around the outside of the cake, and mark it by lightly scoring the cake with a knife. Set the ruler aside.

4. With the knife in one hand and your other hand flat on top of the cake to keep it steady, use a smooth sawing motion to slowly cut around the cake from the outside edges toward the center until the knife is all the way through.

Filling Cake

No matter how many layers your cake will be, you always want the filling layers to be about half as high as your cake layers. I typically do four layers of cake with three layers of filling to achieve tall, beautiful slices. Take time to fill and chill the cake properly in order to avoid what I call the cake "muffin top." That's when the layers of filling haven't been done properly or the filling is too soft for the weight of the cake, causing the cake to get those unsightly little bulges between each layer.

If you're filling the cake with a buttercream frosting only, spread or pipe the buttercream (using a large round decorating tip size #789 or similar) on top of the first cake layer and stop 1/4 inch away from the edge.

When you place the next round of cake on top, press down starting from the center and moving out toward the edges—this forces the buttercream to fill in the space without going over the edge. Repeat with each cake layer until all the layers have been stacked. Use the level to check that the top and sides of your cake are straight.

How to use a softer filling

1. If adding a softer filling like jam or cream cheese frosting, pipe a dam around the top outer edge of the cake round with a firm-setting buttercream.

2. Fill the center with the filling, and top it with the next cake round. Place the cake in the fridge, and allow it to set completely, at least 2 hours but up to overnight, before finishing.

SAVE THAT CAKE TOP!

If you don't immediately give in to the temptation of snacking on the little domed piece of cake you just cut off, you can use it to create "sand" or "dirt" for your next cake design. Dry the cake scraps in oven on low heat (about 250°F for 20–30 minutes). When the cake dome has cooled, run it though a food processor with a few pulses. Store the cake sand in an airtight container (it should last for about a month).

Mini Cakes & Cake Pops

THERE IS NOTHING more ADORABLE THAN TEENY CAKES, BUT THEY REQUIRE A SLIGHTLY different technique than larger cakes. So allow yourself more time when decorating, since you're working with multiple small surfaces. To make mini cakes, use a mini mold or follow the instructions below. Bake cake pops in molds or according to the directions at right.

Mini Cakes

1 batch of cake batter (see Recipes pp. 192–197)

Two parchment-lined half-sheet pans

6 cups firm-setting filling

1 cup buttercream for the crumb crust

1. Divide the batter in two shallow parchment-lined half-sheet pans and bake for 10 to 12 minutes at 350°F. Cool the cakes in the pan for about 30 minutes.

2. Once completely cooled, invert the cake pan to remove one of the cakes—leave the parchment paper on the cake. Place the cake pan upside down on the work surface. Place the cake, parchment side down, on top of the inverted pan.

3. Top the cake layer with a firm-setting Swiss meringue buttercream filling (see recipe for Vanilla Swiss Meringue Buttercream, p. 198). Softer fillings will not allow the mini cakes to hold their shape when cut.

4. Place the other sheet of cake on top of the filling-covered cake with the parchment side up. Peel the parchment off what is now the top of the cake, and spread a thin layer of buttercream over the entire cake. This isn't the crumb coat; it's a trick to help keep the cake from crumbling when it's cut into mini cakes. Refrigerate the cake for up to 2 hours, allowing it to chill completely before being cut. Use a knife or cutters to cut the cake. Then crumb-coat the cakes and cover with fondant.

NOTE: *If you don't plan to fill the mini cakes, bake one cake in a deep, parchment-lined half-sheet pan. Allow it to cool. Invert the cake, remove from the pan, and peel off the parchment. Lightly cover it with frosting, and chill it before cutting it in to shapes. Then crumb-coat the cakes and cover with fondant.*

IF USING A MINI MOLD

- Keep an eye on baking time. Mini molds bake faster.
- Cool the minis in the pan for 20 minutes before unmolding to keep them from crumbling when turned out.
- Refrigerate them once they're unmolded—they are easier to work with when cold.
- Slice and fill them as you would a larger cake.

Cake Pops

One 8-inch round cake, baked and cooled

1/4 cup frosting

12 oz. bag of candy melts (any color)

1-inch ice cream scoop or 1/8-cup measuring cup

Parchment-paper-lined cookie sheet

Medium-sized microwave-safe bowl

Twenty-four 6-inch lollipop sticks

Block of Styrofoam™

1. Use your hands to break the cake into large pieces. Place the pieces in the bowl of a stand mixer fitted with the paddle attachment (or in a large bowl using an electric hand mixer), and mix on low for 3 to 5 minutes to break up the cake pieces into chunky crumbs.

2. With the mixer on low, add the frosting, a spoonful at a time; let it completely combine before adding the next spoonful. The cake mixture should hold together when formed.

3. Use an ice cream scoop or measuring cup to portion the cake mixture. Roll the portions between your hands to form them into balls. Place the balls on a parchment-paper-lined cookie sheet while you finish shaping the rest of the mixture. Place the cookie sheet into the fridge, and allow the cake balls to chill uncovered for at least an hour.

4. Place the candy melts into a medium-sized microwave-safe bowl and microwave on medium power for 30-second intervals until melted. Stir between intervals.

5. Remove the cake balls from the fridge. Hold a cake ball in one hand and use the other hand to dip the tip of a lollipop stick about 1/4 inch into the melted candy melts and then insert the dipped tip into the cake ball until the melted candy is no longer showing. Re-shape the ball with your hands if needed. Stand the cake pop upright in the styrofoam and continue creating the rest of the cake pops. If the candy melts start to set, microwave them again for 10 to 15 seconds and stir.

6. Once all of the balls have been placed on sticks, start with the first pop and dip the cake ball into the melted candy. Turn the lollipop stick to make sure the ball is entirely coated. Gently tap the stick against the side of the bowl to knock off any excess candy. Place the stick back into the Styrofoam block. Candy melts will set at room temperature in about 20 minutes. Place them in the fridge if you want them to set faster.

7. If you want to add sprinkles or sparkles to your cake pops, do it while the cake pop is still wet so the topping adheres to the candy. Just hold the pop over a parchment-lined cookie sheet and sprinkle with the topping.

The Crumb Coat

ONCE YOU'VE GOT THE CAKE SPLIT, LEVELED, AND FILLED, YOU NEED TO CREATE A smooth exterior. Whether the look you want is a casual buttercream finish or an elaborate fondant-covered one, it all starts with the crumb coat.

This layer of buttercream does a few things for the cake: It seals the cake layers, which keeps the cake moist; it keeps crumbs from getting caught in the finish; and it gives the cake a smooth finish to which you can add details. Sometimes the crumb coat is called a "dirty ice," because it catches the tiny crumbs from the cake. Getting a perfectly smooth finish takes practice and patience! I wish there were some sort of supersecret cake magic trick here, but really, it just takes practice.

Troubleshooting a crumb coat

If you're having lots of trouble getting a cake smooth, or are starting to see too many crumbs in the buttercream, the cake has probably been out too long or the buttercream is a little too soft. This is a sign to put down the spatula and stop battling the cake. Take the buttercream out of the piping bag and put it in a bowl. Put the cake and buttercream back in the fridge. Take a breather! For how long? That depends on how soft the buttercream has become and how much time you need away from the cake to recover!

After the buttercream has firmed up in the fridge, bring it back to a fluffy consistency by whipping it at medium-high speed with a whisk attachment on a stand mixer or with a hand-held mixer. The amount of time it takes to bring the buttercream back to a workable consistency will also depend on the heat of your kitchen. You'll know the buttercream is ready when it is pale in color and holds its peaks. Then try the crumb coat again. After you've finished the crumb coat, place the cake in the fridge for at least an hour.

Smoothing the crumb coat

When the crumb coat has set, place the cake on the turntable and hold a long, straight-edged metal spatula vertically against the cake. Spin the turntable and let the spatula gently scrape the frosting to remove any bumps or ridges. Slide the blade of the spatula across the top of the cake for a perfectly smooth top. For larger cakes, you can even use a large putty knife from your local hardware store. Just be sure to use it only for cakes and not for projects around the house!

WHY CRUMB-COAT?

- It seals the cake layers and keeps them nice and moist.
- It catches tiny cake crumbs and keeps them from getting caught in the fondant or buttercream finish.
- It creates a smooth base on which the fondant can adhere.

How to pipe a crumb coat

I find it's much easier to pipe buttercream onto the cake than to scoop it out of a bowl. Using a larger piping tip allows for better coverage and saves time.

1. Use a large, smooth basketweave tip (size #789 or similar) to pipe horizontal strips of frosting around the sides of the cake until it's covered. Cover the top of the cake by piping circles starting at the outer edge working your way towards the middle.

2. Use a metal spatula to smooth the sides of the cake first.

3. After smoothing the sides of the cake, there will be some ridges along the top edge. Hold the spatula horizontally and pull the frosting from the outside edge in toward the center of the cake.

Pull up slightly with the spatula to remove the excess buttercream. Place the cake back in the fridge and allow it to set completely for at least an hour before decorating it.

MAKE *it* BETTER

It's always easier to remove extra frosting than to add more frosting to cover bare areas. So if you're just starting out, use more buttercream than you think you need.

Buttercream Details

FOR AN EVERYDAY OCCASION, THESE BUTTERCREAM techniques can help transform a simple cake into a stunner! Most of these techniques involve using a pastry bag with a tip, with the exception of the rustic finish. They can also be used to easily dress up basic cupcakes. The general kind of tip used for each technique is listed, but play with size to create different kinds of designs. Mix techniques for beautifully textured cakes. The ideal buttercream to use with these techniques is Swiss meringue buttercream (see p. 198), but American buttercream will work as well.

I know that using canned frosting can be tempting when you're in a pinch, but your piping efforts will be wasted because it doesn't hold its shape. It's engineered to remain soft and spreadable so it can be used straight off the shelf. If you must use canned frosting, the rustic technique will work well with it.

RUFFLES

Using a leaf tip (size #68 or #69), hold the piping bag next to the side of the cake so that the widest part of the tip is parallel to the cake. Apply gentle pressure to the piping bag and pipe the buttercream with a back-and-forth motion around the sides of the cake. Move the tip of the piping bag up and down, toward and then away from the surface of the cake. For tighter ruffles, make your back-and-forth motions very quick. You can apply the ruffles horizontally around the cake, or vertically like stripes. The leaf tip gives you a very ripply ruffle with lots of movement.

PEARLS

Rounded Pearls Using a round tip, place the point of the tip directly over the area on the cake where you want to put the pearl. Apply gentle pressure to the pastry bag until you see that the pearl is about half the size you want it to be, then gently reduce the pressure on the pastry bag as you pull the tip away from the cake. For a perfectly rounded pearl, dip your finger in water and gently round over the point left by the piping tip. This technique is the same no matter the size tip you use. Smaller tips, like #1 through #4, will create tiny pearls. Larger tips, like #9 through #12, will create chunky, marble-sized pearls.

Pressed Pearls Any size round tip from #9 through #12 will work well with this technique. Pipe a row of pearls vertically up the side of the cake. Then, using a small metal spatula, pull the pearls horizontally across the cake. Start the next row in the center of the "smear" you created. Continue piping and smearing the pearls all the way around the cake, and finish with a row of pearls.

RUSTIC

No tip needed here! You should still begin with a crumb-coated cake to ensure complete coverage. Next, add another layer while the buttercream is soft. Create lines by dragging the tip of the spatula through the buttercream on your cake. Pull the tip of the metal spatula around the sides of the cake horizontally, or pull straight up and down for rustic stripes. Use the back of a spoon for a home-spun swirly look.

RIBBONS

Using a basketweave tip (smooth or ridged; sizes #46 through #48 work best), pipe a horizontal strip around the top edge of the cake. Pipe the next strip so that it overlaps the last one by a few centimeters. Repeat the pattern down the entire cake for the look of layered ribbons.

SHELLS

Use a star tip to create a shell. Squeeze the piping bag with firm pressure as you start, creating a bump, and release the pressure as you gradually pull away from it to create a thinner tail. Where you apply more pressure, the shell will be thicker, and where you apply less pressure, the shell will be thinner. Pipe the shells in a line if you want to create a border, or cover the cake in shells for a modern, fun look. Tip sizes #21, #22, #32, and #199 all work well with this technique.

ROSETTES

Using a size #30 or #35 star tip, create a rosette by starting in the center of where you want the rosette to be. Applying steady, gentle pressure, pipe a swirl around that point in a clockwise motion. Use your nondominant hand to steady the hand you're piping with, if necessary. When you reach the end of the rosette, let up the pressure and pull the piping bag away following the edge of the rosette. Create a dramatic effect by covering an entire cake in rosettes, or create individual rosette cupcakes.

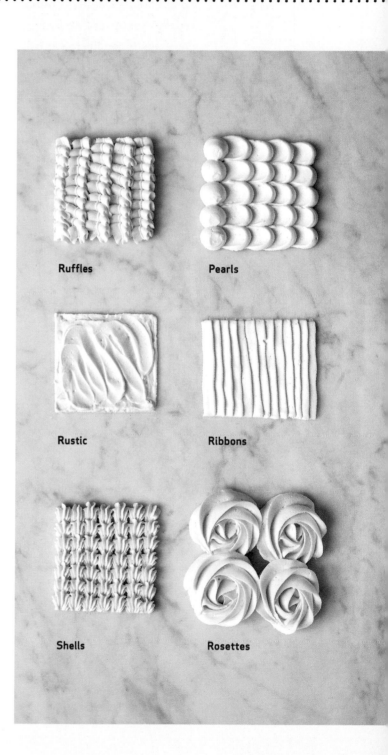

Ruffles

Pearls

Rustic

Ribbons

Shells

Rosettes

Fondant Finish

TO ACHIEVE A SMOOTH FONDANT FINISH, YOU WANT TO START WITH A SMOOTH, CHILLED, crumb-coated cake. Applying fondant rarely helps cover up buttercream blemishes—it can actually amplify the mistakes when the fondant settles into them.

Fondant has to be applied to a cake that has been completely chilled in order to achieve sharp edges. If the cake is still soft, the result will be rounded and puffy in appearance. When applying fondant, only a firm-setting crumb coat will do—a whipped cream or boiled frosting will be way too soft to work with. There are many kinds of fondant available. I use Satin Ice® fondant for its beautiful smooth texture and mellow taste. If you'd prefer to make your own, try the easy Marshmallow Fondant recipe on p. 208.

Start by kneading the fondant until it's completely uniform and smooth in texture. (Kneading store-bought fondant activates the gums in it.) If it's not kneaded enough, fondant will be more likely to crack and separate. If the fondant is a little too sticky when you are rolling it out, dust the work surface with cornstarch. If the fondant is a little dry, lightly rub the work area with vegetable shortening.

MAKE *it* BETTER

Lightly spray your cake with water or brush it with piping gel before applying the fondant. This helps it better adhere to the cake's surface, which prevents air bubbles from forming.

How to apply fondant

When you want to cover a cake with fondant, use this method—it's the most popular.

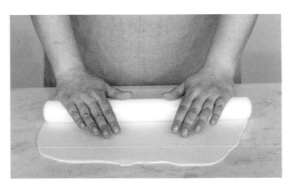

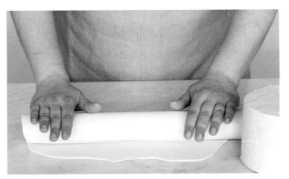

1. Start with a ball of kneaded fondant and flatten the top with the palm of your hand. Using a smooth plastic rolling pin, roll the fondant from the center out to the sides until it's about 1/4 inch thick. Trim the edges of the fondant to roughly match the shape of the cake being covered so that it is easier to handle.

2. Wrap the edge of the fondant closest to you around your rolling pin and roll it away from you until the entire piece is wrapped around the pin.

3. Hold the pin on the side of cake farthest from you and unroll it toward you to drape the fondant across the top of the cake.

4. Smooth the top of the cake flat with your hands, and press the fondant securely around the top edge of the cake to prevent the fondant from tearing as it hangs down.

5. Work from the top down to smooth the fondant onto the sides of the cake. As you spread the fondant down the sides of the cake, gently pull on the bottom of the fondant to prevent it from creasing.

6. Run your fingernail or the dull side of a knife around the bottom edge of the cake to create a sharp seam. Apply enough pressure to create a crease, but not enough to pierce the fondant. Using an X-ACTO knife, scalpel, or paring knife, trim away the excess fondant around the base of the cake.

7. To smooth the fondant finish, place one smoother on top of the cake and the other vertically on the side of the cake. For the top of the cake, run the smoother along the surface of the cake in a gentle back-and-forth motion. For the sides of the cake, move the smoother in an up-and-down motion. Use gentle, steady pressure. Don't press so hard that the fondant tears or moves around on the cake.

FAST FIX!
If tiny cracks form (ones that are not large enough to start over, but large enough to drive you crazy), smooth a tiny bit of vegetable shortening over the crack to help bring the seam together.

Pieced fondant

The piecing method is a great way to cover an oddly shaped cake or to get sharp corners on a square or a sharp top edge on a round cake. For a cleaner look, the top is covered first and the top seam is hidden when the side piece (or pieces) of fondant is (or are) placed. Any excess fondant is trimmed away before the cake is smoothed.

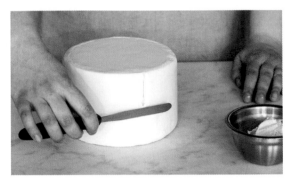

1. Roll out a piece of fondant large enough to cover the top of the cake with a little overlap. Place the fondant onto the cake and smooth it to the edges with your hands. Use a sharp knife to trim the fondant away from the side so that the piece covers the entire top (see photo above left). Run your finger around the cut edge to help smooth out the cut.

2. Roll out a piece of fondant as wide as your cake is tall, and long enough to wrap around the cake once. (This is where the circumference chart comes in handy; see p. 25.)

3. Roll up the fondant strip into a spool. Place the edge of the strip against the side of a round cake (or at a corner if you're covering a square), and unroll the fondant strip around the cake as you press it to the sides of the cake.

4. Smooth the fondant using your hands, and trim the top and side edges so that they are flush with the cake.

5. Smooth the fondant finish using fondant smoothers as described in Step 7 in the instructions for how to apply fondant (p. 23).

6. If you're piecing fondant on a round cake, hide the seam where the fondant comes together by tinting the buttercream so it's close in color to the fondant. Use a metal spatula to spread some of it over the seams (see photo above right). Wipe away the extra buttercream with your finger or a damp paper towel.

With the seam filled it will be less noticeable, but I still tend to use that side as the back of the cake. You can also cover the seam with fondant decorations or by piping a line of buttercream pearls or shells over it.

MAKE *it* BETTER

Fondant hates moisture and humidity! Always start with dry hands and a dry work surface. It's easiest to cover a cake in fondant in an air-conditioned room.

FONDANT COLOR

Many times in cake decorating, designers focus on using shapes and complicated techniques, but color is the best way to add drama with little effort. When using color as a design element, always start with bright, saturated colors, because it's easier to mute a color than to build one up.

Most food coloring packaging will include a color chart with recommended color ratios; use it to create the color you need. To color the fondant with gel food coloring, create a well in the center of the fondant. Use the manufacturer's recommended amount, and begin to fold and knead it into the fondant until the color is uniform. If the fondant is sticky, dust your work surface with a little cornstarch. If the fondant is dry, try rubbing the work surface with a very small amount of vegetable shortening to moisten it. If you are coloring a white fondant, wrap it in plastic wrap once colored and allow it to rest before rolling it out to use it.

Most brands of fondant work best with gel colors; an exception is Fondarific®, which is best colored with powdered colors that are specially made for tinting candy or chocolates.

Many fondants come precolored, which helps save time and elbow grease. The hues achieved in the chart below were created by adding white, black, or brown fondant to ready-made fondant colors. I used Satin Ice, but you can use the product of your choice.

Create different hues by adding white, black, and chocolate fondant (top to bottom left) to ready-made fondant colors (across the top).

How to find the cake circumference

Math has never been my strong suit. In fact, even the word "circumference" kind of makes me start to sweat. But in cake decorating, math is very important for planning how much of something you'll need or how many of a decoration to make.

To find the circumference of your cake, the equation is $C = \pi \times$ diameter. To simplify, let's round Pi to 3.14. To save you from breaking out the calculator, here is a quick chart with the circumferences of common round cake sizes rounded up to the nearest inch.

CAKE ROUND	CIRCUMFERENCE
6 in.	19 in.
8 in.	26 in.
10 in.	32 in.
12 in.	38 in.
14 in.	44 in.

Doweling & Stacking

DOWELING A CAKE HELPS GIVE YOUR CREATION THE OH-SO-IMPORTANT STRUCTURE IT needs. Whether buttercream or fondant finished, I dowel every tiered cake. Even just one dowel supporting a 4-inch round on top of a 6-inch round is a little piece of security that ensures your cake will end up looking exactly the way you want it to when it gets to its destination. Every cake in a tiered cake should be finished on a cardboard cake round. The cardboard rounds sit on the dowels in the cake below, creating a structure that will keep your cake in place.

The best dowels are round plastic ones, which can be purchased anywhere cake decorating supplies are sold, or wooden dowels, which can be found at a cake supply store or hardware store. Wooden dowels can be easier to find, and they come in different diameters, which allows mixing and matching the dowels to the cake's size and support needs. The round plastic dowels made for cakes are lighter than wood and made to support a good deal of weight. I use either depending on the size of cake that I'm working on.

Placing dowels

To figure out how long the dowels should be, insert a dowel into the center of the cake and mark where it starts to stick out of the cake. Remove it and cut all the dowels for that tier to that size. If you are using thicker dowels, it's better to first measure the depth of the cake using a wooden skewer and cut the dowels to the depth marked on it. Measuring first with a thin skewer will prevent you from making too many large holes in your cake. (Remember: Do not use the skewer as a dowel—it won't hold the cake!)

When you are placing dowels in the cake, start with the bottom tier. Use an odd number of dowels as you work your way up the tiers of the cake, and place them in opposite spaces. For example, for a three-tier cake, you'd start with five dowels in the bottom tier: one in the center and four around it (see Figure 1). Make sure that the four dowels are placed within the diameter of the tier that will sit above it. A great way to mark the next tier is to place that size cake pan on top of the tier you're working on, and use a knife to lightly outline the pan.

After inserting the dowels into the first tier, spread buttercream or royal icing over that area so that the cake board under the next tier will adhere to it. You want to use enough icing so that the next cake will stick, but not so much that it oozes out the sides when the tier is applied. (If any icing does ooze out, just use a clean, dry paintbrush to lift the extra away.)

For the next tier (on a three-tier cake), use three dowels. Place them into the second tier in a triangular shape so that they sit in spaces opposite where dowels below them sit—as if you're building a mini Eiffel Tower within the cake. Keeping the dowels opposite each other from tier to tier gives the cake more balance. If all of the dowels lined up from tier to tier, you'd have large sections of cake in between the dowels with nothing supporting it. To finish the cake, place the final tier on top, and then you're ready to decorate it.

Doweling tall cakes

To stabilize cakes that are taller than three tiers,
consider using a long center dowel through the entire
cake *after* you have stacked it—this means you can
skip placing the center dowel in the cake when you
are stacking it, but you will still need to use the outer
dowels. First, cut the dowel to match the height of
the cake. Then use a sharp knife to trim one end of
the dowel to a point so that it will pierce the
cardboard rounds as it is pushed through the cake
layers. Next, take a deep breath and press the dowel
through the center of the cake from the top down.
When you hit the cardboard rounds, use a mallet—or
even your rolling pin—to gently tap the top of the
dowel to help it through. Stop when the dowel hits
the cake base.

Fill in the hole on the top of the cake left by the
dowel with a little bit of buttercream or cover it with
a decoration that matches the cake. Always allow the
cake to set completely before moving it. Don't move
a freshly stacked cake before the icing between the
tiers has set, or your cake tiers will slip and slide.

If you've used buttercream between the tiers, put
the cake back in the fridge for at least an hour to
make sure it's secure. Royal icing will set quicker at
room temperature, which makes it a good option for
warmer weather.

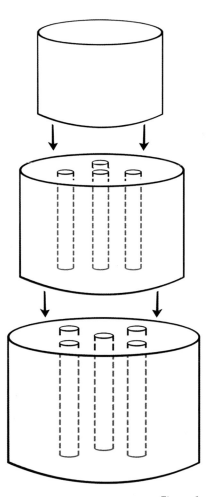

Figure 1

It's All in the Details

YOU'VE TAKEN THE TIME TO PATIENTLY BAKE, SPLIT, FILL, AND crumb-coat the cakes and now it's time for the really fun part—decorating! Great cake decorating starts with mastering a few relatively simple techniques. I've shared some of them in this chapter, because they are the ones that are most frequently used throughout the rest of the book. Once you master these basic skills you'll be able to combine and layer techniques to create new designs. Play with size, color, shape, and scale for new twists on traditional design elements. Patience and practice are key as you learn each new technique.

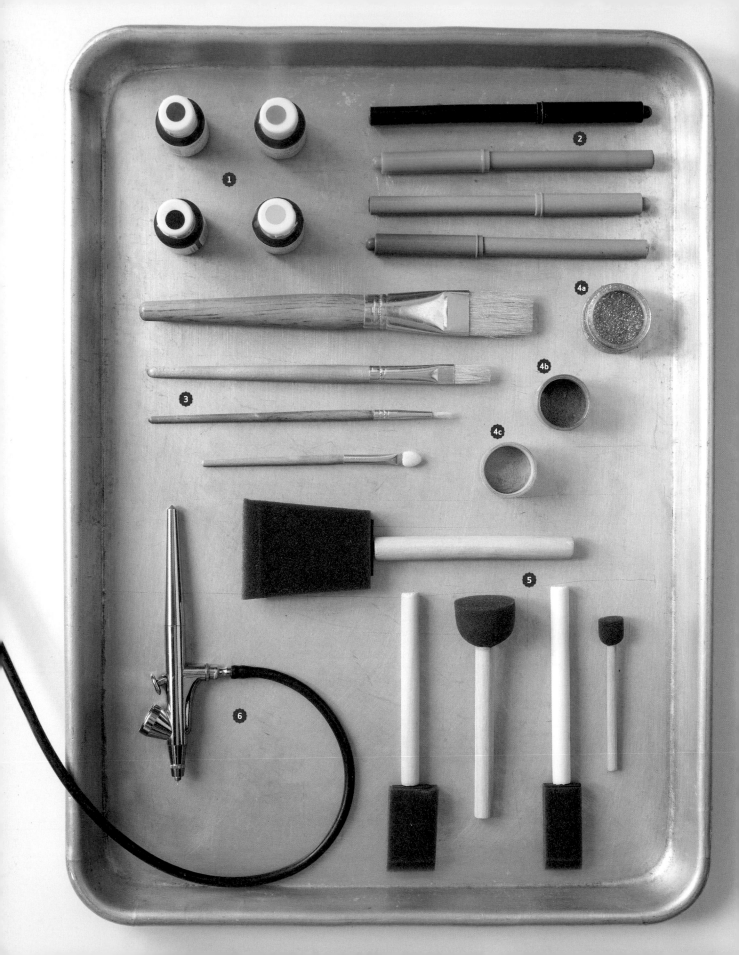

Adding Color

PLAYING WITH COLOR IS A QUICK AND EASY WAY TO TURN A PLAIN CAKE DESIGN into something extraordinary. I love using it as a design element.

1. Gel food color

I only use gel colors because they yield the best and brightest results. Another perk is that you need less gel color (as opposed to the supermarket liquid colors) to get great results, which means less moisture is added to your fondant.

2. Food-color markers

Food-color markers come in a wide variety of sizes and colors. They're a great tool for writing a message on fondant. I prefer the felt-tipped type for a darker, smoother line. Storing them with the tip down will help them last longer.

3. Paintbrushes

It's always good to have brushes in a variety of shapes and sizes. I prefer to use white-bristled synthetic brushes, because they let me see the color and how much of it is on the brush, before I apply it.

4. Dusts

These are powdered colors that can be applied dry for an opaque finish, or mixed with vodka or any clear extract (like lemon extract) for a more paint-like consistency. Vodka and extracts are used because they evaporate quickly, leaving only the color behind.

a. Disco dust makes a cake sparkly! Because dusts are heavier they can be applied using a dab of piping gel.

b. Luster dusts have a metalic sheen. They are great for creating realistic-looking, satin-like ribbons and bows. I prefer to brush luster dust on dry for the best shimmery effect. Painting it on will give you a more solid metallic look.

c. Petal dusts are matte powders perfect for coloring gum paste flowers. Real flowers are made of shades of color, so petal dusts work great to achieve depth and lightness where needed.

5. Foam craft brush

Foam brushes found in craft stores are handy for applying color to stamps, or directly on cakes when you want a watercolor-style effect. They can also be used with food coloring to create a sponge-painted look, which is great for stonelike or antique finishes.

6. Airbrush

This is definitely an investment tool, but with practice, it yields fantastic results. It's great for tinting leaves and flowers, as well as for shading.

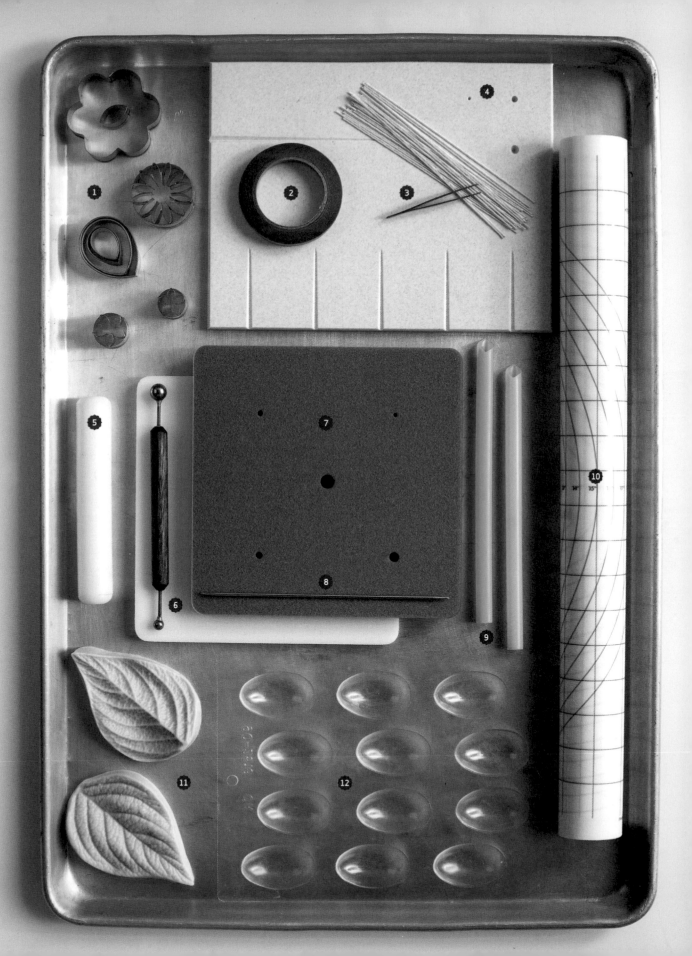

Flower-Making Tools

MAKING GUM PASTE FLOWERS IS A SKILL THAT TAKES TIME TO DEVELOP, BUT INVESTING in the correct tools will get you started on the right foot.

1. Flower petal cutters
Start with a rose petal set, which will allow you to create a variety of different flowers and leaves. Then expand your collection to include peonies, orchids, dahlias, sunflowers, stephanotis, and others.

2. Floral tape
Used for covering wire on a finished flower or taping petals together, it is not really sticky like regular tape. The stickiness is activated as you pull and wrap it around the wire.

3. Covered floral wire and tweezers
I use white wire because it is easily tinted, so it's the most versatile. Wires also come in different gauges. The lower the gauge number, the thinner the wire. I purchase 22-gauge wire in straight bundles that are about 6 inches long. Tweezers help bend the wire ends.

4. CelBoard
It is used for creating wired flowers and leaves or for making a Mexican-hat-style flower.

5. Small fondant roller
A small 6-inch plastic rolling pin is great for working on small decoration projects.

6. Ball tool
This allows you to smooth edges and create thinner petals. The metal ball tool is better than a plastic one. It rolls more smoothly and is typically less likely to stick to fondant or gum paste.

7. Foam mat
It gives you a solid but springy surface when using the ball tool to thin petal edges. The little holes are helpful when making a Mexican-hat-style flower.

8. Knitting needle
Great for folding over the edges of rose petals, creating creases, placing small decorations on cakes, and so on.

9. Floral picks or straws
It's generally frowned upon to place wires directly into your cake, so attach the wires to floral picks or place them within straws.

10. Plastic mat
Plastic mats offer a smooth surface on which to roll and cut gum paste. Any plastic placemat will do.

11. Veiner
I always keep two in my kit. One is a multipurpose leaf press, which works well for adding realistic textures to both gum paste and fondant leaves. The other is a silicone press made by molding a piece of lettuce out of silicone.

12. Egg trays or crates
Egg tray molds used for candy making also come in handy for drying flower petals and other decorations. Foam egg crates help to shape petals as they dry. Having both on hand will give you more options for drying different decorations.

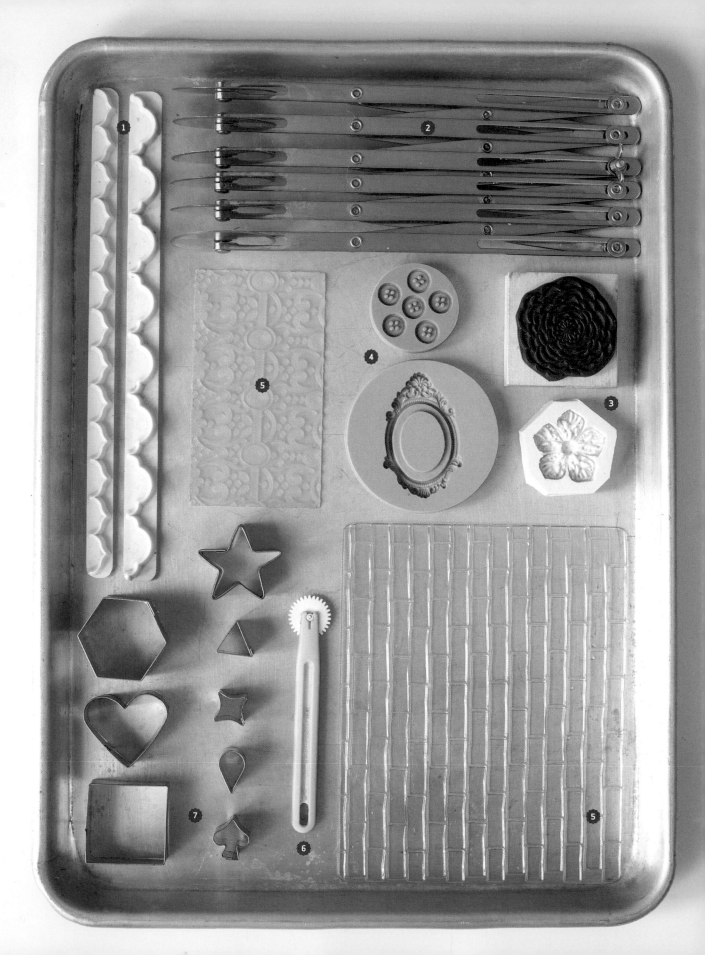

Tools for Texture & Shape

TEXTURE AND SHAPE TOOLS ARE USED TO CREATE MOST OF THE DESIGN WORK ON THE cakes in this book. These tools help take your cake designs to the next level, because adding texture to any design instantly adds dimension and creates a more polished look.

1. Border cutters

These are used for creating different borders or trims. They can also be used to add pretty edges to your ribbons and bows.

2. Accordion cutter

This is an investment tool, but it's something I recommend picking up if you plan to make many wedding cakes—or lots of cakes with ribbons or bows. The accordion cutter allows you to cut multiple strips of fondant of the same size all at once. If you don't want to invest in an accordion cutter, a ruler and a pizza cutter or sharp knife will do the trick.

3. Stamps

Any kind of stamp can be used in cake decorating. Traditional wood-mounted rubber stamps work especially well on flat surfaces. Newer clear plastic "cling"-style stamps are great to have as well, because they are flexible and easy to bend around the edges of a cake. If your stamp has been used with regular ink, don't use it on a cake—always keep your cake stamps separate!

4. Molds

Silicone molds are a fantastic way to add great dimension to your cake details with minimal effort. As with all your tools, keep the cake molds separate from the ones you use to mold clay or anything else. Molds can be found in all shapes and sizes. Lace, buttons, shells, bottles, and more can all be made using silicone molds. Look for molds at craft and cake decorating supply stores. There are also terrific online resources.

5. Textured mats

These come in all shapes and sizes. The most useful mats are often the simplest ones, because they can be used to create different textures and patterns. Diamond patterns, dots, stripes, and animal prints are some of the most common. I frequently use a simple floral scroll mat to add depth to ribbons and bows.

6. Quilting/docking tool

This tool creates a docked, or quilted, line when rolled over fondant or gum paste. Find one that comes with a few different interchangeable wheels so that it's more versatile.

7. Cutters

The very first set you should buy is a good set of simple round cutters. (Ateco is my brand of choice. Their cutters come in a storage tin, which helps keep them protected, organized, and easy to find.) You will be surprised how many times you'll find yourself using a circle as a starting point for a pattern or design. Some other handy basic shapes include squares, ovals, hexagons, and diamonds.

Simple Fondant Details

HERE IS WHY I LOVE FONDANT OH-SO-MUCH! BY MASTERING A FEW EASY DESIGN SKILLS, you can create anything—that still blows my mind. You can look at a shape, break it down into its simplest forms, and then recreate it, in layers, by using the appropriate techniques. So many complicated-looking designs are just simple techniques repeated or layered. Here are a few of the most common techniques used in cake decorating, and the ones I use most frequently in the cake patterns later in the book.

Shapes

These are probably the easiest fondant details to create.

Fondant (or 50/50 Mix; see sidebar on p. 37)

Plastic rolling pin

Cutter or template

Sharp knife

Cornstarch or vegetable shortening

TO MAKE CUTOUT SHAPES

1. Start by rolling fondant to the thickness called for in the pattern, or to $1/4$ inch thick.

2. Cut out the shapes using cutters or using a template and a sharp knife. If the fondant is sticky, dust it with cornstarch. You can also dip your cutter in cornstarch or rub it lightly with vegetable shortening to ensure the fondant doesn't stick to the cutter.

3. Once the shape is cut, look for tiny frayed edges on the fondant. Trim away the frays with a sharp knife, or run your finger along the edge of the shape to smooth it out.

4. If you want the shape to be freestanding, allow it to dry overnight (approximately eight hours). If applying it directly to the cake, brush the contact point with a little water or piping gel—use water if the piece is light or piping gel if the piece is larger or heavier.

CREATE A MESSAGE BOARD

A fun use for fondant shapes is creating plaques on which to paint, draw, or write messages. Cut the desired shape out and leave it to dry overnight. Use a food-color marker to write your congratulations or happy birthday message in your best penmanship on the fondant plaque. Be sure your fondant is completely dried first. If you try to write on soft fondant, the surface of the fondant may pull or tear.

50/50 Mix

To give raised decorations even more stability, use a blend of 50% fondant to 50% gum paste. The gum paste will help the decoration dry firmer, so it doesn't lose its form. Tylose or CMC (carboxymethyl cellulose) can also be added to fondant to help it dry faster and firmer. Tylose and CMC both come in powder form and can be found at cake decorating supply stores or online. Add either to the fondant according to the manufacturer's instructions—it's usually about a teaspoon for every two pounds of fondant.

Cut Fondant Flowers

Once you've mastered cutting shapes, you can turn them into flowers.

Fondant (or 50/50 mix; see sidebar above)

Plastic rolling pin

Cutter or template

Sharp knife

Cornstarch or vegetable shortening

TO MAKE FLOWER CUTOUTS

1. Roll the fondant so that it's ¼ inch to ⅛ inch thick.

2. Cut the flower shapes with cutters or using a template and a sharp knife. If the fondant is sticky, dust it with cornstarch or dip your cutter or knife in cornstarch or vegetable shortening.

3. For an appliqué-style look that lies flat against the cake, immediately apply the flower to the cake with a bit of water or piping gel that has been brushed onto the cake in the spot where you want the flower to go.

4. To make a flower come away from the cake, add dimension by placing it in a lightly greased egg cup to dry overnight before adhering it to the cake. If you don't have egg cups, you can shape the flowers by placing them in egg crates or a cup made from aluminum foil. Larger flowers will need more drying time than smaller flowers. Drying time will also vary depending on how humid the kitchen is. If you want to add a color, paint or dust the flowers once they are dry.

5. Apply larger dried flowers with piping gel or buttercream. Smaller dried flowers can be affixed with water. Pipe the flower centers with buttercream or royal icing, or use a tiny ball of fondant, depending on the look you want to create.

MAKE it BETTER

Be creative when drying out your flowers! Add dimension and shape by curling petals over dowels or rolling the ends with a knitting needle. Look at pictures of real flowers and try replicating the way their petals fall.

Puffs

These puffs are a simple way to make flowers. Make them using fruit leathers, as shown, or make them from fondant or gum paste as done in The Graduate cake design on p. 112.

Fruit leather (or fondant or gum paste)

Round cookie cutters (1/2 inch to 2 inches in diameter)

Small block of Styrofoam

Floral wire (toothpicks or skewers would also work)

TO MAKE THE PUFFS

1. If you're using fruit leather, unwrap one, remove it from the plastic backing, and cut out six circles. If you are using fondant or gum paste, roll it out to about $1/8$ inch thick. It should be large enough to cut out six circles of whatever size cutter you're using.

2. Pick up a circle with both hands, and using your thumbs and forefingers, pinch the sides of the circles together towards the center to create a shape resembling a ruffled X. Just be sure you don't close the X entirely—the open loops are what give the puff its shape. Repeat the step with the other five circles. I use six circles for a full-looking puff. You can use more or less depending on how full you'd like the puff to be.

3. To begin to form the puff, press two of the ruffled circles together at their points. If the fruit leather or fondant has begun to dry out, brush on a small amount of water so that they stick together. Add more ruffles until you achieve the desired puff shape.

4. Set the formed puff onto a piece of Styrofoam. Use floral wire or toothpicks to prop up the fruit leather puff into its desired shape. Allow the puff to dry out for at least two hours, but ideally overnight so it holds its shape. Drying time may vary depending on the humidity in your room. Using the wires or toothpicks helps to keep the puff from drooping or losing its shape as it dries.

5. Fruit leather puffs can be applied using water or piping gel. Fondant or gum paste puffs will be a little heavier, so apply them using royal icing or buttercream.

Ribbon

Ribbons are another simple technique that can be enhanced in a number of ways.
They are the foundation for creating bows and ribbon roses.

Fondant (or 50/50
Mix; see p. 37)

Plastic rolling pin

Knife and ruler or
accordion cutter

TO MAKE THE RIBBON

1. Roll out the fondant to the thickness called for in the pattern, typically $^1/_4$ inch or
$^1/_8$ inch thick.

2. If you are using the accordion cutter to cut the ribbon, set the cutter to the desired
width and roll the cutter over the surface of the fondant to cut it. If you are using a
ruler and knife to cut the ribbon, gently place the ruler on the fondant and mark the
width you would like the ribbon to be. Then use the ruler as a guide to cut the ribbon.
Be careful not to press on the ruler so hard that it marks the fondant.

3. To pick up the ribbon, carefully roll it up into a spool, starting at one end of the
ribbon—almost like a roll of tape. Don't roll it too tightly. You want to be able to
easily unroll it onto the cake.

4. Brush the surface to which the ribbon will be applied with a small amount of water
or piping gel, and unroll the fondant ribbon onto the cake. Applying ribbon to a cake
is easiest if you have the cake on a turntable. That way, you can hold the ribbon level
with one hand while spinning the turntable with the other, which helps apply it
smoothly around the cake.

5. If you want to apply ribbon around the top or middle of cake, use painter's masking
tape or a ribbon to create guidelines. Use the edge of the tape or ribbon as your guide,
and then gently remove it once the fondant ribbon is set in place.

MAKE *it* BETTER

If the fondant feels sticky, lightly dust the surface
of it with cornstarch before cutting. Dip the knife or
pastry cutter in cornstarch between each cut,
as well. Be sure to wipe the knife so that it is clean
and dry before each pass. Any bits of fondant left
on the cutting tool will stick to the rolled fondant
and cause tearing.

Bows

Once you've mastered making ribbons, you can move on to making bows.

Fondant ribbon
(see p. 39)

Fondant (or 50/50
Mix, see p. 37)

TO MAKE THE BOW

1. Start by creating a ribbon that will be as wide as the thickest part of the bow and twice as long as you want the loops of the bow to be. Cut the ribbon in half widthwise into two equal strips.

2. Pinch the corners at the end of one strip, and then press both corners in toward the center pinched point. Repeat at the opposite end, and do the same to the second strip.

3. To create the loop, fold the pinched ends together. For an open loop on a large bow, bring the pinched ends together around a rolling pin; on a smaller bow use a dowel. Allow the loops to dry out overnight or for a few days. Make sure they are thoroughly dried before using them so that they don't lose their shape.

4. To assemble the bow, place two loops end to end. Roll out a small strip of fondant and cut it into a strip that's long enough to wrap around the ends to hold them together. Apply it to the cake using water or piping gel.

5. If you want to assemble the bow directly onto the cake, once the loops have dried, brush a little water, piping gel, or buttercream onto the cake where you wish to apply the bow. Gently press the individual loops onto the fondant covered cake with the pinched ends facing each other.

6. Fill in the space between the loops with a small ball of fondant to create the center knot. Score the ball with the back of a knife or knitting needle to give the illusion of folds.

7. If you'd like the bow to have tails, cut two extra strips that are the same thickness as the bow loops. Pinch at one end and cut the other end in a V or diagonal line. Attach the pinched ends to the center of the bow loops before applying the knot. If you have cut the ends on a diagonal, make sure the shorter sides are facing in.

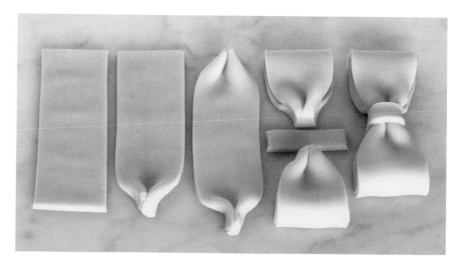

Ribbon Roses

This is a quick and easy rose-making method based on the ribbon technique. It's great for beginners or time-pressed decorators.

Fondant ribbon
(see p. 39)

Knife

TO MAKE THE ROSES

1. Start by creating a ribbon that's about $1/4$ inch thick and twice as wide as you'd like the height of the rose to be. The longer the ribbon, the wider the finished rose will be. It's always easier to start with a longer ribbon than you think you'll need rather than end up being short.

2. Fold the ribbon in half horizontally, but do not create a hard seam.

3. Start at one end, and roll up the ribbon so that the rounded side will face out. Depending on how you'd like the flower to look, you can roll the ribbon up smoothly (as shown) or you can pinch it along the way to create a more ruffled looking rose.

4. Use a sharp knife to trim the back of the flower flat, about $1/4$ inch from the top of the rose, so that it will lay smooth when pressed against the cake. Trim the rose higher or lower depending on how you want it to sit on the cake.

5. Apply the flower using a little bit of water if it is small. If it's larger, you may want to use buttercream or royal icing.

Ruffles

Turn ribbons into ruffles, and add texture to your cake with this fabric-inspired look. Ruffles are a great addition to cakes inspired by dress details.

Fondant ribbon
(see p. 39)

Toothpicks (optional)

TO MAKE THE RUFFLES

1. Cut a fondant ribbon as described on p. 39. Cut the ribbon to your desired width, and with a length about five times longer than you want the finished ruffle to be.

2. Begin at one end and gently create an accordion fold down the length of the ribbon. The more folds you create, the more ruffles the ribbon will have.

3. Leave the ruffled strip as is and apply it immediately to the cake with piping gel or royal icing. Or pinch the ruffle together on one side to create a fan shape. You can leave it out to dry overnight for use as a cupcake topper or to apply to the cake upright.

4. To add to the fluffiness of the ruffle, prop the loops open with toothpicks. Allow it to dry overnight or for at least an hour.

MAKE *it* BETTER

When leaving any fondant decoration out to dry, be sure to keep it in a dark, dry place. Colored fondant fades easily when exposed to direct sunlight. Do not refrigerate fondant decorations while they are drying out. Refrigerators have a level of humidity in them that will actually start to soften dried decorations.

Draping

The ribbon's thickness will have a big effect on the size of the folds in the drape. The thicker you roll it, the fewer the folds you'll have. The thinner you roll it, the more folds you'll be able to create.

Fondant ribbon
(see p. 39)

Parchment paper or
plastic mat

TO MAKE THE DRAPE

1. Cut a fondant ribbon as described on p. 39. Cut the piece of fondant as wide as you'd like the drape to be and about four times longer than you want the drape to hang.

2. Lay the ribbon horizontally on your work surface, and accordion-fold it from top to bottom. Keep the center lightly folded and pinch the ends.

3. Place the drape on a piece of parchment paper or a plastic mat to dry overnight if you want it to have a rigid shape. For a softer drape that fits the shape of your cake, apply the drape directly to the cake before it has dried. To do this, brush its entire back with water or piping gel so that you're not relying on the ends to secure the weight of the whole drape.

Molds

Silicone molds are an excellent tool for creating intricate cake decorations.

Fondant (or 50/50 Mix; see p. 37)

Paintbrush

Vegetable shortening

Silicone mold

TO MOLD FONDANT

1. Start by lightly brushing the inside of the mold with a tiny bit of shortening. If you can see the shortening, there is too much, so remove some by wiping out the inside with a paper towel.

2. To create evenly molded pieces, roll the fondant (or 50/50 Mix) into a ball that is approximately the same size as the inside of the mold. Press it into the most detailed part of the mold first, then flatten out the fondant through the rest of the mold by firmly pushing and pressing it into all other areas. Trim away any excess fondant.

TO MOLD FLOWERS

1. If you're molding something very thin, like flowers, roll out the fondant (or 50/50 Mix) first so it's approximately $1/8$ inch thick. Use flower cutters that are the same size as the mold to cut the flower shape.

2. Place the fondant on the mold and press it between both pieces of the mold. Gently remove the molded flower. If you'd like more dimension, you can place it in an egg cup to dry. Molded pieces can be allowed to dry out completely (drying time depends on the size of the piece) or the pieces can be applied to the cake right away. Apply molded pieces by brushing the back with water or piping gel before pressing onto the cake.

FAST FIX!
Sometimes shapes can become warped as they're moved from the cutting table onto a cake. If that happens, gently press the cutter onto the shape that's been placed on the cake. Trim away any misshapen parts with a sharp knife.

Cake Stamping

Stamping a pattern onto a fondant-covered cake is a quick and simple way to make your own patterns or give your cake a hand-painted look.

Gel food color

Small bowl

Foam brushes

Stamps

TO STAMP THE CAKE

1. Squirt a small amount (about the size of a grape) of gel food coloring into a bowl. Work with small amounts of color at a time so that it doesn't dry out.

2. Use a foam brush to add a thin coating of color to the stamp. (The foam brush ensures even coverage.) You want enough color so that the outline of the stamp comes through clearly, but not so much that you get thick smudged lines.

3. Press the stamp onto the surface of the cake, applying firm, even pressure. Apply enough pressure to create the pattern without breaking the surface of the fondant. If you're working with a flat stamp against a rounded surface, gently and steadily roll the stamp over the surface of the cake. If it's your first time using the stamp, try it first on a piece of parchment paper or fondant rolled flat on the table. Play with the amount of color you add until you get the desired effect.

4. Add more color to the stamp before stamping again. If your stamp starts to accumulate color, rinse it with water and dry thoroughly before beginning again. For more on painting the stamped image, see the sidebar on p. 107.

Cake Painting

WHILE YOU COULD ADD COLOR TO A CAKE BY WAY OF COLORED FONDANT, SOME techniques require you to add color by painting it onto the fondant or gum paste. Flowers, for example, look much more realistic when you can capture the varying tones of a petal, and simply painting color into a stamped cake (as in the Craft Cake on p. 104) can also really add some extra "wow" factor.

There are various ways to paint a cake, and getting good at it requires practice and patience, but I can offer a few hints that I hope will help you along. The first thing to remember with any coloring method is to apply paint sparingly in stages and allow it to dry before adding the next layer of color—too much paint at a time will run and cause your fondant to get sticky. If it does run, gently wipe away the paint with a damp cloth. Allow the fondant to dry before painting again. For smaller mistakes, remove paint with a cotton swab or a small paintbrush dipped in vodka.

Gel food colors are my first choice for painting on fondant. When used right out of the container, they are very thick and can be a little difficult to spread, so thin them with a little bit of vodka or clear extract for a paint-like consistency. If you happen to thin the gel color too much, wait a little while for the vodka to evaporate, and the paint will thicken. I also use gel colors to add detail to gum paste flowers. Because gel colors are more solid, they work well for adding tiny dots on stamens or the edges of petals using a small paintbrush.

Airbrush colors are thinner than gel colors so that they can flow freely through the airbrush nozzle. Because of this you won't need to thin colors before you start painting with them. When working with an airbrush machine always read the manufacturer's instructions before using it. It's important that you thoroughly clean and dry the airbrush after each use to keep the machine working properly and prevent the nozzle from sputtering or clogging. And always keep in mind that the color is airborne! Set up a backdrop behind the cake (I use a cardboard box) to avoid getting the color all over your house. If you're planning to airbrush a large cake or lots of decorations, make sure your room is well ventilated and wear a painter's mask or surgical mask so you don't inhale the color. If you'd like, you can apply airbrush colors with a paintbrush when you want more of a brush-stroke watercolor effect. If using a paintbrush, you can add petal or luster dusts to the airbrush colors to thicken the paint and create new colors.

Petal or luster dusts can be brushed on to fondant and gum paste dry or wet. Petal dusts will create a paint that dries to a matte finish, while luster dusts will dry with a more shimmery finish.

When painting flowers, petal and luster dusts are my first choice. I like to start flowers with a white or very lightly colored gum paste. Once the gum paste petals are dry, I add color by dry-brushing dusts onto them. Applying the color dry allows me to better create lighter and darker tones throughout the same petal, just like a real flower. Once you get the color you desire, use steam to set the color. Create the steam with a clothes steamer or a pot of boiling water, then gently move the flower in and out of the steam (but don't let it touch the water). This takes just a minute to do. The petals will appear glossy when the color is set, then turn matte again after they are dry.

Gum Paste Flowers

GUM PASTE FLOWERS—ALSO KNOWN AS SUGAR FLOWERS—ARE WHAT MADE ME FALL IN love with cake decorating. Before I learned how to make them in a class taught by famed cake decorator Ron Ben Israel, I was really unsure of my direction in the dessert world. I loved working as a pastry chef, but felt there was something missing. After the class, I knew that what had been missing was the artistic outlet that creating gum paste flowers provided.

Making gum paste flowers is truly an art form. I love how fragile and delicate they are. There's something so romantic about spending the time to create something that eventually disappears. And when I feel like I've totally had it with cake decorating (yes, it even happens to me; it usually lasts a minute or two and is typically brought on by something breaking), gum paste flowers are what keep me coming back.

Creating gum paste flowers can be a time-consuming process, but it becomes faster with practice. When kept cool and dry, gum paste flowers last for a very long time. I still have some of the first ones I made. Start the flowers at least a week in advance of when you want to use them in order to give yourself time for drying, coloring, wiring petals together, and—of course—to allow for breakage. Oh, the sound of petals shattering on the floor! I know it all too well. But there's no crying over broken flowers.

There are three basic methods for creating gum paste flowers: glued petals, wired petals, and the Mexican Hat Method. These are each basic starting points that you can build on over time and as you accumulate more tools. Any flower can be created using one or more of these techniques.

Glued Petals

This technique can be used to create many kinds of flowers, but it is most commonly used to create roses. Once the petals have dried, they are glued on in layers. The end product is solid, and it can't be adjusted once it has dried. It's a great method for beginners, because it can be done without any special tools.

Simple Rose

22-gauge floral wire

Tweezers

$1/4$ pound of gum paste

About 1 Tbs. of gum paste glue (see sidebar on p. 50)

Rose petal cutters

Foam mat

Ball tool

Knitting needle

Small paintbrush

Piece of Styrofoam or wire rack

Petal dusts

Calyx cutter

TO MAKE A SIMPLE ROSE

1. Bend the tip of a floral wire into a small hook using a pair of tweezers. It's important to start with the wire bent so that it anchors into the gum paste. Roll a grape-sized piece of gum paste into a teardrop shape. Dip the bent tip of the wire in gum paste glue, and insert it into the widest part of the teardrop. Allow it to dry solid.

2. Roll about an ounce of gum paste very thin on a flat surface. Working in small batches like this keeps the petals from drying out.

3. To make the center of the rose, cut two petals using the smallest cutter in the set. On a foam mat, thin the edges of the petals with your ball tool. Thin just the very edges of the petal, not the whole thing. Place the petals in front of you so that the pointed ends face down. Using a knitting needle, roll back the upper right hand sides of the petals, to create a little curl. Brush a small amount of gum paste glue onto the pointed lower half of both petals. Apply them to the dried center with the pointed ends facing down. Tuck the curled edges of the petals together so that they interlock, mimicking the shape of the center of a tightly curled rose. Allow this to dry until firm, at least an hour.

4. Next, roll another ounce of gum paste in the same manner as above, and cut out three petals with the cutter that's the next size up. Curl the petal in the same way you curled the first two, but this time, flip them over and apply the gum paste glue to the base of the other side, opposite the curl. Press the first petal onto the center, curl side out. Now, working counterclockwise, apply the next petal so that the curled edge overlaps the flat edge of the petal that was just placed. When you get to the last petal, gently lift up the edge of the first petal so that you can tuck the flat edge under that first curl. Allow it to dry until firm. For drying, place the end of the wire into a piece of Styrofoam, or bend the wire stem of the rose and hang it on a wire rack.

MAKE *it* BETTER

Perfectly rolled gum paste should be so thin that you could read a newspaper through it. But getting gum paste to roll this thin will take some experience. Beginners, try to get it as thin as you can while still being able to work with it.

5. Continue to cut and layer the petals this way, creating more petals by working your way up the cutters in the set. Each petal layer should increase by an odd number (three, five, seven, etc.). Remember to give the petals shape and dimension by rolling back the edges around a knitting needle (a thin dowel also works) before letting them dry.

NOTE: *The farther apart you place the petals, the more open the flower will look. For a closed rose, wrap the petals tightly around the center.*

6. Add color at this point by brushing the rose with petal dusts. For a more solid-colored rose, start with gum paste a shade or two lighter than the color you want the rose to be. Then go back in with petal dust after the rose has dried to add dimension to the color.

7. After the rose has been colored, create the calyx (the leafy green base to the rose). You can purchase a calyx cutter or use a small five-petaled blossom shape, like a stephanotis cutter. Roll out a quarter-sized piece of green gum paste so it's paper thin and cut it with the calyx cutter. Brush one side with gum paste glue. Insert the rose's wire into the center of the star with the glued side facing the rose. Slide the shape up the wire, and press it onto the underside of the rose. It's these little finishing touches that add to the flowers' realism.

Wired Petals

Wiring flower petals is a very popular flower technique. The center and each petal are created on individual floral wires, which allows greater flexibility when decorating because each petal can be adjusted. The method can be used to create peonies, tulips, anemones, and orchids. The peony method shared below is used on the Toile cake on p. 136. Because the petals are created one at a time, it can take up to an hour to make all that you'll need for the peony (see photo on p. 47). It may take more or less time depending on your skill level and experience. It's a skill that becomes faster with practice.

Wired Peony

16 pieces of 22-gauge floral wire (one for the center and then one for every petal)

Tweezers

$1/4$ pound of gum paste

About 1 Tbs. gum paste glue (see sidebar below)

Paintbrush

CelBoard

Peony petal cutters

Foam mat

Ball tool

Lettuce leaf mold (optional)

Egg tray

Floral tape

TO MAKE A WIRED PEONY

1. Bend the tip of one floral wire into a small hook using a pair of tweezers. It's important to start with the wire bent so that it anchors into the gum paste. If the wire were kept straight, it could slip out when the gum paste dries, causing your beautiful bloom to drop to the floor (*shudder*).

2. Form a ball out of a grape-sized piece of gum paste. Shape the ball with your hands into a fat teardrop shape. This is the center of the peony. Dip the bent part of the floral wire into the gum paste glue and insert it into the teardrop. Allow it to dry solid, at least 1 hour. If you plan to turn it into a bud or closed flower, wrap the wire with green floral tape at this time. You do not need to wrap the wire if you are continuing on with the full peony.

3. Roll out about 1 ounce of gum paste on a flat surface or on your CelBoard. Roll the gum paste very thin, so that it is almost translucent. Cut out 3 peony petals using the smallest cutter in your set. Place the petals on a foam mat and thin all the edges using a ball tool.

4. Brush a small amount of gum paste glue onto the base of each petal. Apply the petals to the bottom of the center—near the wire—one at a time, overlapping the edges of each petal clockwise. At the end, lift up the edge of the first petal and slide the last petal underneath. Allow the petals to dry solid (at least an hour). This will be the center of your peony, to which all the other petals will be wired.

GUM PASTE GLUE

To make gum paste glue, combine 1 cup of tap water with a quarter-sized amount of gum paste. Allow the gum paste to dissolve in the water for 10 to 15 minutes. Gum paste glue can be stored in the fridge for about 3 weeks.

5. Create at least 15 more peony petals with the medium and large cutters in your set, more if you want a very full flower. Roll about an ounce of gum paste flat across the grooves of a CelBoard, then flip the gum paste over so that the little channels are facing up. When cutting out the petal shapes, the channel created by the groove should run vertically through the center of the petal.

6. Dip a floral wire in gum paste glue and gently push it into the channel starting at the base of the petal. Push the wire a little less than an inch into the petal.

7. Place the petal on a foam mat and roll the edges with a ball tool until they are thinned out and slightly frilled. The more pressure you apply to the ball tool, the frillier the edges of the petal will appear. For added texture, you can press the petal in a lettuce leaf press before thinning the edges.

8. Hold the petal at its base and bend the floral wire so that it's easier to place in an egg tray to dry overnight. Allowing the petals to dry in an egg cup will give them a more natural shape.

9. When the peony center and wired petals have dried, use floral tape to tape the petal wires to the center wire. Work from the smallest petals out to the largest. If you are wiring a flower together for the first time, it might be easier to tape one petal at a time. Hold the petal wire up against the center wire so that the base of the petal meets the base of the center. Starting where the petal and center meet, wrap the wires together using floral tape working your way down the wires. Tape them close enough to each other so the petals overlap at the edges, similar to a real flower. With more experience you'll be able to wrap multiple petals to the center at a time.

10. How you color your petals will depend on what you want your finished flower to look like. For a soft, translucent look, assemble your flower before lightly dusting the edges with color. For a brighter, more solid look, paint each petal after it has firmed up and allow the color to dry before assembling the flower.

Mexican Hat Method

Yes, it really is called the Mexican Hat Method! Why? Because the little piece of gum paste you create to make a flower looks like a teeny, tiny sombrero. This technique is most commonly used to create small filler-style blossoms like stephanotis or jasmine.

Stephanotis

1 ounce gum paste

CelBoard

Small plastic rolling pin

Five-point blossom cutter

Foam mat

Ball tool

Tweezers

22-gauge floral wire

$1/4$ cup gum paste glue (see sidebar on p. 50)

Piece of Styrofoam or wire rack

TO MAKE A STEPHANOTIS

1. Roll a small gumball-sized amount of gum paste into a ball. Place it over the CelBoard's cone-shaped indentation, and roll it flat with a small rolling pin. Roll the gum paste as thin as you want the finished petals to be—ideally, that's nearly translucent.

2. Carefully, remove the gum paste from the CelBoard and flip it over onto a flat surface, exposing the new, little cone-shape lump created by the board.

3. Using a small five-point blossom cutter, cut out the shape using the lump to mark the center of the flower.

4. Place the blossom bump side down on a foam mat and use the ball tool to press into the center of each petal to give it a concave shape.

5. Use tweezers to make a hook at the end of the floral wire. Dip the hooked end of the wire in gum paste glue, and from the top of the flower, insert the wire into the cone shaped center of the flower so that the hooked end is last to enter the flower. Do not pull the hook all the way through the flower. Push the petals up slightly, and allow the flower to dry solid. Push the end of the wire into a piece of Styrofoam or bend the wire to hang it over a wire rack to dry.

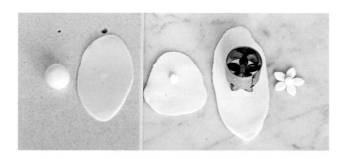

Inspiration

INSPIRATION IS A FUNNY THING. FOR ME, IT SEEMS TO BE ABUNDANT WHEN I HAVE LITTLE time to act on it and sometimes elusive when I need to come up with a new design. For this reason, I keep a list of things that inspire me.

In my phone I have a running list of cake ideas that I add to whenever they come to me. I used to keep a paper inspiration journal, but having my phone with me all the time enables me to record an idea when it comes to me—and they sometimes come at the strangest times! Inspiration can strike while flipping through a new catalogue or magazine, or when simply taking a walk down the street.

When inspiration strikes, the tool to execute such inspiration isn't always readily available. Creating a template is a great way to add to the custom nature of a cake. Templates can be created from anything—leaves, flowers, toys, jewelry, paper goods, and more. They are also useful when you can't find the shape you need as a cutter. A template will help keep a design consistent every time it's used.

When choosing the material to create a template, keep in mind how you'll be using it. If it needs to be able to bend around the sides of a cake, use something thin and flexible, like parchment paper. If cutting multiples of the same shape, use something sturdier, like poster board. If you create a template that you'd like to use more than once, you can even have it cut out of wood by a carpenter. There are also companies online that will turn your template into a cutter. This can get pricey, but if it's

something that you know you will use often, it can be a great time-saver.

Besides templates, silicone molds are also a terrific tool to use when bringing a design to life. Molds can be purchased online or in many cake decorating supply and craft stores. You can even make your own molds using food-safe silicone molding compound, which can be found on cake supply Web sites. Most compounds work in a similar way and are very easy to use, but you should always follow manufacturer's instructions. Usually, they come in two parts that you combine to activate the molding compound. Some compounds are liquid and can be poured over an object to mold. Other compounds are kneaded together like clay and can be shaped around an object to create a mold. I love to create custom molds for my cake designs. Jewelry, toys, buttons, shells, and more can all be used to create beautiful, reusable molds. Once you make your first mold, you'll be hooked!

The important thing to remember is that it's okay to be creative and have fun. The designs in the book are meant to inspire you. You can follow my directions and designs or mix and match the techniques to make designs of your own. Once you get started, there's no telling what you can accomplish!

PART TWO

DECORATE LIKE YOU MEAN IT

Nature Inspired

WHEN SEARCHING FOR INSPIRATION, LOOK NO FURTHER THAN
the world around you! Natural elements like leaves, trees, and animals
provide an endless source of ideas for all kinds of events. Using natural
elements in cake decorating is nothing new, but the ideas in this chapter
explore some of those elements in an updated and more modern way.

Make It Pretty Basics

Here are some tips that will help you with the cakes in this chapter.

- All of the cakes in this book are made up of four cake layers (baked in two pans and split in half), unless otherwise instructed.

- Use a brush of water to adhere fondant. Heavier pieces may require using piping gel, buttercream, or royal icing.

- In warmer months, working in an air-conditioned room is best. Finished cakes should be stored in the fridge overnight, or at room temperature if being served that day.

Hills & Bales

MY FAVORITE PART OF LIVING IN NEW ENGLAND IS DRIVING THROUGH THE COUNTRYSIDE in the fall and seeing golden rolled bales of hay dotting the green grassy hills. It's so idyllic—so beautiful—that I just had to create a cake design based on it. This design would work great for a quirky, rustic wedding; add a small toy barn and a cow or two in the background, and it's a modern take on a child's birthday cake. The hills are made by using varying shades of green fondant: I like to use chartreuse, Kelly green, and forest green.

FOR THE CAKE

6-inch and 10-inch round cakes, filled and crumb-coated (pp. 14–15; pp. 18–19)

$3^1/2$ pounds light green fondant

2 pounds medium green fondant

$4^1/2$ pounds dark green fondant

12 ounces yellow fondant

4 ounces brown fondant

Round cutters (ranging from 1 inch to $2^1/2$ inches in diameter)

Piping gel or buttercream

Cake-Making Tools (p. 10)

FOR THE MINI CAKES

Six 3-inch round mini cakes, crumb-coated (see Mini Cakes on p. 16)

$1^1/2$ pounds yellow fondant

$1/2$ pound brown fondant

Round cutters (ranging in size from $1/4$ inch to 3 inches in diameter)

Parchment-paper-lined cookie sheet

TO MAKE THE HILLS

1. Cover the 6-inch round cake with $1/2$ pound of the light green fondant according to the directions on p. 22. Cover the 10-inch round cake with $2^1/2$ pounds of the dark green fondant in the same manner. Dowel and stack the cakes according to the directions on p. 26.

2. To create the hills, roll out $1/2$ pound of the dark green fondant into a rectangle that's about 19 inches long by 4 inches wide and $1/8$ inch thick. Cut the top of the rectangle lengthwise in a wavy line to create hills and valleys. Gently roll up the strip into a spool.

3. Brush the 6-inch cake lightly with water and unroll the hilly strip around it so that the tallest hill is about an inch away from the top edge of the cake. The flat edge should be parallel to the bottom of the cake. Use a knife to trim the strip where the ends meet, creating a seam on the side of the cake. Gently trim the hills where the strip meets so that they match up.

4. Repeat Steps 2 and 3 for the same tier using the medium green fondant, but roll the fondant rectangle so that it is 19 inches long by 3 inches wide and $1/8$ inch thick. Place the medium green hills about 2 inches from the top edge of the cake. Repeat Steps 2 and 3 again with the light green fondant, but cut the strip so that the highest hill is no taller than 3 inches high and place it so that its bottom edge lines up with the bottom edge of the tier.

continued

5. For the bottom tier, use the same method as described in Steps 2 through 4, but make these strips at least 32 inches long so they wrap all the way around the cake. Start with the medium green fondant and make the highest hill no taller than 5 inches. The next strip, light green, should have hills no taller than about 3 inches. The third strip, dark green, should have hills no taller than about $2^{1}/_{2}$ inches. And the last strip, medium green again, should have hills no taller than 2 inches. If it's difficult for you to work with a strip so long, cut the strips in half and start the seams at the sides of the cake so they aren't visible from the front—or you can just plan to place hay bales where the ends meet. Get a little creative when placing your strips, and allow them to peak, valley, and overlap. Try not to line things up symmetrically or you'll lose the natural look of the cake.

6. Finish the bottom edge of your top tier by rolling the leftover medium green fondant into a rope about $^{1}/_{4}$ inch in diameter and 19 inches long. Wrap the rope around the base of the top tier; adhere with water if needed. Later, cover the seam with one of your hay bales.

TO MAKE THE HAY BALES

7. Knead the yellow and brown fondants together to create a marbled fondant. The goal is to have streaks of yellow and brown, not to create a new solid color.

8. Roll out the marbled fondant into a rope about $^{1}/_{4}$ inch in diameter. Coil the rope into circles that are about $2^{1}/_{2}$ inches in diameter. Use a $2^{1}/_{2}$-inch round cutter to sharpen the edges of your coiled circles.

9. To create the look of rolled, baled hay, center the 2-inch round cutters onto one of the fondant circles and gently press firmly enough to create lines, but not so hard that it cuts all the way through. Repeat the process using all of the smaller cutters. Repeat for all of the fondant circles.

10. To adhere the circles, brush the back of each one with a little bit of piping gel or buttercream and stick them randomly on the cake. Since they are thick and heavy, water will not hold them as well.

TO DECORATE THE MINI CAKES

1. Marble the yellow and brown fondants as in Step 7 for the hay bales, and divide the fondant into six pieces.

2. Use a rolling pin to roll one of the pieces of the marbled fondant into a 6-inch circle, about ⅛ inch thick.

3. Cover the mini cake using the instructions on p. 22 and use a knife to trim away any excess fondant.

4. Create the hay bale lines on the top of the mini cake using the circle cutters, as described in Step 9 for the hay bales. Press the cutters into the top of the mini cake firmly enough to create lines, but not so hard that they cut all the way through. Use the back of a knife to gently mark the sides of the mini cake with horizontal lines, and you're done.

MAKE IT *or* FAKE IT!

In a pinch, use puffed rice cereal treats to create mini hay bales. Make them on your own, or purchase premade treats. Premade cereal treats are easily molded by hand into rounds or squares. Cover them with a thin layer of frosting, and roll them in toasted coconut for a supereasy, but still tasty, bale of hay. If you want to cover your rice-treat hay bale in fondant, first dip it in melted chocolate—this will take the bumps out of the rice treat. Then cover it in fondant according to the mini cake instructions.

By the Sea

I CREATE CAKES FOR WEDDINGS UP AND DOWN THE COAST OF NORTHERN NEW ENGLAND, so I'm asked to make ocean-themed cakes all the time. It's a good thing I love the ocean! It's such a terrific source of inspiration. I couldn't imagine living anyplace other than costal New Hampshire. I know the sea isn't for everyone, so if you're more of a lake person, you can create the waves in this cake in more muted blues and swap out the shells for smooth river stones and lake grasses.

FOR THE CAKE

6-inch, 8-inch, and 10-inch round cakes, filled and crumb-coated (pp. 14–15; pp. 18–19)

$9^1/2$ pounds white fondant

6 pounds blue fondant (start with Satin Ice baby blue or teal color)

Various molded gum paste shells (see molding technique on p. 44)

$2^1/2$-inch round cutter

Paintbrush

Cake-Making Tools (p. 10)

TO MAKE THE WAVES

1. Cover the cakes with 6 pounds of the white fondant using the method on p. 22, and dowel and stack the cakes according to the directions on p. 26.

2. To create the three shades of blue that you'll need for the waves, combine the blue and white fondants in the proportions on the wave color chart (see p. 64).

3. Roll out the lightest blue fondant to a strip that's 32 inches long by $4^1/2$ inches wide by $1/4$ inch thick.

4. Using a ruler, measure and mark the fondant with a knife every $2^1/2$ inches lengthwise.

5. With the round cutter, cut out half-circles along the top of the strip, using the marks as a guide.

6. Roll up the wave strip into a spool. Brush the bottom cake tier with water and unroll the wave strip around the sides of the cake. Trim away the excess fondant at the seam.

7. Repeat Steps 3 through 6 for the middle blue shade and the darkest blue shade for the 10-inch cake, using the same width for each wave strip but reducing the length for each shade according to the chart on p. 64. Follow these instructions and the chart on p. 64 to make wave strips for the 8-inch and 6-inch cakes.

8. To keep the points of the waves in line, start each wave strip on a point; that way when you line up the next one you'll always be starting at a point. For a "surfer" style wave, gently

continued

Wave color chart

	DARK BLUE FONDANT	WHITE FONDANT
Darkest blue	3 pounds	none
Middle blue	2 pounds	1 pound
Lightest blue	1 pound	2 pounds

Fondant wave strip measurements

	6-INCH ROUND CAKE	8-INCH ROUND CAKE	10-INCH ROUND CAKE
Lightest blue wave strip	19 in. long × 4^1/$_2$ in. wide	26 in. long × 4^1/$_2$ in. wide	32 in. long × 4^1/$_2$ in. wide
Middle blue wave strip	19 in. long × 3 in. wide	26 in. long × 3 in. wide	32 in. long × 3 in. wide
Darkest blue wave strip	19 in. long × 1^1/$_2$ in. wide	26 in. long × 1^1/$_2$ in. wide	32 in. long × 1^1/$_2$ in. wide

SMALLER SHINDIGS

This design would translate wonderfully to smaller servings:

- Make a single-tier cake for a smaller event. On a single cake, the sugar shells would work best on the top to finish it and fill that space.

- Bake cupcakes in blue wrappers, frost them with white Swiss meringue buttercream, and roll the tops of the cupcakes in blue sanding sugar. Finish them by topping the cupcakes with molded fondant shells; be sure to use fondant shells and not ones made from gum paste. Fondant is softer and will be easier to eat as part of a cupcake.

knock the peaks over so that they're all pointing to the side in the same direction.

TO DECORATE THE CAKE

1. Make the nautical rope for the center tier by dividing the remaining ^{1}/$_2$ pound of white fondant in half.

2. Roll each piece of fondant into a rope that's about ^{1}/$_4$ inch in diameter.

3. Line the two ropes up next to each other and pinch them together at the ends. Hold an end in each hand and twist the ropes together.

4. Lay the rope onto the cake around the middle tier. Place the rope so that the ends will be hidden by your shells.

5. Place the molded gum paste shells in clusters around the cake as you like. With this kind of application, I prefer to rest the shells on the cake as they would lay naturally, as opposed to applying them flat against the sides. Gum paste dries very hard, which will help the shells keep their shape but will make them less than desirable to eat. Be sure to remove them before serving.

Tree Bark & Birds

THIS VERY REALISTIC BARK TECHNIQUE IS SURE TO FOOL ALL OF YOUR GUESTS! WHAT appears to be a tree stump with cute little chirpy birds on top is really a delicious layered cake. Though it looks complicated, creating the look of bark is actually really easy. This cake is great as a birthday cake. Or, carve initials into the top for a rustically romantic anniversary cake.

FOR THE CAKE

8-inch round cake, filled and crumb-coated (pp. 14–15; pp. 18–19)

2 pounds ivory fondant

2 cups of thick royal icing (see recipe on p. 207)

8 ounces red fondant

4 ounces green fondant

Gel food colors in chocolate brown and forest green

Knitting needle

Black food-color marker

Foam craft brushes

Airbrush and airbrush colors in chocolate brown, forest green, and ivory (optional)

1-inch petal cutter

Extruder (optional)

1-inch leaf cutter

Silicone leaf veiner

Small paintbrush

TO MAKE THE TREE STUMP

1. Cover the cake with ivory fondant using the method on p. 22.

2. Use the tip of a knitting needle to make rings on the top of the cake by pressing gently into the fondant. Start by making smaller rings in the center of the cake and increase their size as you reach the cake's edges. The more random the marks, the better the design, because they will give the illusion of the center of the tree stump. Make a few straight lines from the center of the cake toward the edge. As you make the lines, you don't need to be even or symmetrical. Search the Internet for images of tree stumps to use as a reference. If you want to carve initials into the top of the stump, do so while making the ring and line marks using the black food-color marker.

3. Create the bark by slathering the sides of the cake with royal icing. You can do this with a small metal spatula, or you can use your clean hands. You're not looking for a smooth finish; you want it to be lumpy and bumpy—like tree bark. Then use a small metal spatula to add bark lines. Pull the icing so that it sticks up past the top of the cake and down onto the cake board, giving the top and bottom edges a rough finish just like a stump.

4. Put the cake into the refrigerator and allow the royal icing to set for

continued

at least an hour. If your fridge has a high level of humidity, the icing won't set. In that case, leave the cake at room temperature until the icing has hardened over, about an hour.

5. Once the icing has set, begin the color treatment. Start with forest green. If you don't have an airbrush, place a drop of green gel food color onto a foam craft brush and use the brush to make random green marks around the sides of the cake only. This will help add to the depth of color in the final finish. If you're using an airbrush, spray little dots of green in random places around the sides of the cake.

6. Next, spray or brush the chocolate brown color over the entire cake. Don't make the coating too thick. Use just enough so that the cake is evenly finished in a chocolate brown color. This will be the darkest color in your final product. Let this layer of color set until it's tacky—the color should lose its high gloss.

7. Dampen a paper towel. Starting on top, lightly wipe the surface of the cake in a circular motion with the paper towel— not so hard that you wipe it back to ivory, but just enough so the raised surfaces of the cake are a lighter shade of brown than the tree rings. Wipe the sides of the cake in an up- and-down motion. The direction in which you wipe makes a difference! On the top it adds to the illusion of the tree's rings, and on the sides it gives direction to your tree bark. Use fresh paper towels as needed.

NOTE: *This painting technique may seem a little scary, but trust me—the messier you are, the better! Practice by smearing royal icing on a piece of cardboard and play with the color there first.*

TO MAKE THE BIRDS AND VINES

NOTE: *Birds can be made in advance and allowed to dry completely.*

8. To make the birds, divide the red fondant into two equal pieces. Wrap one in plastic and set aside.

9. To make the first bird, divide the red fondant in half again. With your hands, roll one piece into a ball for the bird's body, then taper the ball at one end so it resembles a plump teardrop. Place the teardrop on its side and set it aside while you make the rest of the bird.

continued

SMALLER SHINDIGS

- The same techniques used for the large cake can be used to create tree stump mini cakes (see instructions on p. 16).
- Make the birds and use them to top freshly frosted cupcakes. When you frost the cupcakes, run the back of a spoon around the top of the cake to create a little swirl, just like the rings of a tree.

10. Divide the remaining fondant in half again. Use your hands to roll one half into a ball to form the bird's head. Brush the rounded end of the bird's body with a little bit of water and set the head on top.

11. Roll out the remaining fondant until it's $1/4$ inch thick. Use the petal cutter to create two wings. To create the tail, cut out a triangle that's $2^1/4$ inches on its longest sides and $1^1/2$ inches at its base. Then cut off the tip of the triangle about $3/4$ inch from the top. Set the pieces aside to dry for at least 30 minutes.

12. While waiting for the bird's tail and wings to dry, make the vines. Divide the green fondant in half. Use your hands or an extruder to roll one half into a rope and create thin vines. Use a rolling pin to roll the other piece of green fondant out to $1/8$ inch thick. Cut out the leaf shapes and add texture lines with the silicone leaf veiner or with a knitting needle. Gently pinch the leaves in half and allow them to bend and move naturally. Apply the vines and leaves to the sides of the cake with a little bit of water if needed.

NOTE: *If the color finish on the cake gets dinged up while you are adding the vines and leaves, don't stress! Just go back in with a small paintbrush and add brown coloring where needed.*

13. When the tail and wing shapes have set, brush a little bit of water onto the areas of the bird's body where you want to apply them. Place the wings with the rounded end toward the front of the bird, and the tail onto the back of the bird so that it sticks up straight. Draw its eyes on with the edible marker.

14. Make one more bird using the remaining red fondant, repeating Steps 9 through 13.

15. Place a dab of royal icing in the tree bark where you'd like the birds to perch. Gently press the bird onto the icing. Use enough to secure the bird, but not so much that it's visible. If any oozes out, brush it away with the small paintbrush. Use the same technique to apply the tiny fondant leaves.

The Wreath

WE ALL HAVE ONE: THE UBIQUITOUS BUNDT PAN. ADMITTEDLY, MINE SAT IN MY KITCHEN, unused, for far too long. Then, while creating holiday desserts for my clients, it came to me. Aha! That little pan looks like a wreath—fantastic! And so this design was born. Bundt cakes are great in their simplicity, so I like to leave this cake unfilled. Because it doesn't have any temperature-sensitive ingredients, it can be left out on a table at holiday parties or taken with you on the road when visiting friends or family.

FOR THE CAKE

8-inch round classic bundt cake

$1/2$ cup seedless jam (a flavor that complements your cake)

3 pounds dark green fondant

2 ounces red fondant, about the size of a golf ball

10-inch round cake base or platter

Pastry brush

Holly leaf cookie cutter (approx. $1^1/2$ inches long)

Small paintbrush

SMALLER SHINDIGS

For a festive handheld option:

- Bake cupcakes in green wrappers and arrange them on a platter in a wreath shape. Top the cupcakes with fondant holly leaves and berries. Guests can help themselves while you enjoy the party without stopping to cut cake!

TO COVER THE CAKE

1. After the cake has cooled, remove any cake that has baked over the edge of the pan to ensure it sits flat when turned over.

2. To keep the cake from sliding on the cake base as you decorate it, brush a small amount of jam onto the base where you want to place the cake. Place the cake so the rounded part is facing up.

3. Use the pastry brush to coat the cake with jam. This helps the fondant stick to the cake and adds flavor.

4. Roll out 2 pounds of the green fondant until it's less than $1/4$ inch thick. Roll the fondant around the rolling pin, and unroll it over the bundt cake to cover it.

5. Starting with the center of the cake, gently press the fondant into the hole. Score the center with a sharp knife and begin to press the fondant down even farther so that it sticks onto the sides of the hole in the cake.

NOTE: *Covering the sides of the hole can be tricky. Don't worry if the fondant tears a tiny bit or doesn't cover it entirely. Blemishes can be covered later with fondant holly leaves.*

6. Once the center is covered, smooth down the fondant on the top of the cake and then around the sides using the same method as for a standard round cake (see p. 22). Trim away the excess fondant, and save it for making holly leaves. Set the cake aside.

continued

TO MAKE AND APPLY THE LEAVES

N O T E : *Don't feel the need to cut out all of the leaves at once. Working in batches helps the work go faster, and also keeps the leaves from drying while they are being applied.*

1. Roll out the remaining green fondant so that it's a little thinner than the fondant used for the cake. Cut out the leaf shapes using a holly leaf cutter (or create a leaf template; see inspiration on p. 53). For added dimension, use the back of a knife to gently score a line down the center of the holly leaves. Make 60 to 70 leaves for an 8-inch bundt cake.

2. To apply the holly leaves, brush a small amount of water (or leftover jam) onto the cake before placing the leaves. When placing the leaves, it's best to start at the top of the cake and work your way down the center hole. Then work about three-quarters of the way down the outer sides so that the tips of the leaves are visible around the outer edges. Overlap the leaves and let them fall in different directions, just like real leaves.

3. For added dimension, dry some holly leaves overnight or for at least an hour. Place those leaves on last, overlapping the tips to create little clusters.

4. To make the holly berries, pinch off a pea-sized piece of red fondant and roll it between your fingers into a ball. Make at least 12 holly berries, or more, depending on how many you'd like on the cake. Brush a small amount of water or jam onto the cake before placing the berries. Holly berries look cute in clusters of three or as single berries. Placing them in odd-numbered clusters helps give the cake a more realistic look.

VARIATIONS

By using different shaped leaf cutters, you can bring this design into any season.

For a festive autumn look: Use oak or maple leaf–shaped cutters, and create leaves in shades of red and orange. Finish it with tiny fondant acorns.

For spring: Cover the cake with classic oval or teardrop-shaped leaves in a paler shade of green, and finish it with tiny fondant blossoms or ribbon roses.

In the summertime: Create a pretty floral wreath by layering a floral shape, like daisies, in various colors. Finish the wreath with a few bright green fondant leaves tucked between the flowers.

MAKE *it* BETTER

Bundt cakes can sometimes have a rounded edge at the base (depending on how much cake you trimmed away at the start). In that case, after covering the cake with fondant, I use the back of my knife to push the fondant under the edge of the cake. This helps to give the cake a cleaner finished appearance.

White on White

I LOVE THE IMPACT OF A MONOCHROMATIC FINISH! IT'S SO GRAPHIC AND BOLD. THIS LOOK is spectacular as a wedding cake or an elegant birthday cake. The white-on-white look can be created with any seasonal elements—snowflakes, leaves, flowers and vines, etc. A key to this cake is preparation. Creating the elements ahead of time makes for a much faster and frustration-free assembly. You can make them up to a week in advance and store them in an airtight container in a dark, dry place. Another key to the success of this design is texture. In the absence of color, texture adds depth and interest.

FOR THE CAKE

1 pound 50/50 Mix (see p. 37)

6-inch, 8-inch, and 10-inch round cakes, filled and crumb-coated (pp. 14–15; pp. 18–19)

$6^{1}/_{2}$ pounds white fondant

1 cup royal icing (see recipe on p. 207)

Cake-Making Tools (p. 10)

2-inch- and 1-inch-wide butterfly cutters

Knitting needle

8 x 11 card stock or poster board

2-inch- and 1-inch-long leaf cutters

Silicone leaf press and flower press (optional)

Aluminum foil

$1^{1}/_{4}$-inch-long rose petal cutter

1-inch five-petal blossom cutter

Plastic egg molds or flower formers

Small paintbrush

Piping tip with a small, round opening (#2 or #3) and piping bag

TO MAKE THE BUTTERFLIES

1. Divide the 50/50 Mix into four pieces. Wrap three of the pieces in plastic wrap and set them aside for later.

2. Roll out the unwrapped piece of 50/50 Mix until it's about 6 inches square and $1/8$ inch thick. Cut out butterfly shapes.

3. Use the tip of a knitting needle to indent the 50/50 Mix where the body of the butterfly would be. Add shapes and lines to the wings, mimicking the details on a real butterfly's wings.

4. Fold the piece of card stock lengthwise into an accordion. Open it up and place the butterflies into the folds. Allow the butterflies to dry overnight or until firm, at least an hour. These should dry the longest so that they maintain their shape.

TO MAKE THE LEAVES

5. Roll out one of the remaining pieces of the 50/50 Mix to $1/4$ inch thick. Cut out the leaf shapes with cutters.

6. Press the leaves with a leaf press to create realistic details, or use the tip of a knitting needle to gently score vein lines onto the leaf.

7. Crumple up a piece of aluminum foil and then slightly open the foil back up, leaving it wrinkled. Place the leaves on the foil to dry for at least 30 minutes. When you place them on the foil, let them droop and fold in random places, just like real leaves.

continued

TO MAKE THE FLOWERS

8. Roll out another piece of the 50/50 Mix until it's about 6 inches by 4 inches and $1/8$ inch thick. Cut out four petals using the rose petal cutter.

9. Place one petal in front of you so that the pointed end is facing you. Use the pointed tip of the rose petal cutter to cut a small V into the top edge of the petal. Press the petal in a lettuce press or use the knitting needle to add texture to the petal. Using a knitting needle, gently roll the top right hand corner of the fattest part of the petal toward you just enough to slightly curl the top of the petal no farther than to the tip of the V. Turn the petal over and place it in an egg mold, rolled side down, to dry. Repeat with the rest of the petals. Create enough petals for seven flowers.

10. To make a bud, start with a small ball of white fondant, about the size of a large pea or a small grape, and roll it in your hands until it's round. Apply more pressure to one side to create a teardrop shape. Make a total of 9 buds.

11. Using the side of a knitting needle, press lines coming from the tip of the teardrop down toward the rounded part.

12. Set the buds aside to dry for at least 30 minutes. You'll finish the flowers directly on the cake.

13. To make the smaller flowers, roll the last piece of 50/50 Mix until it's about 6 inches by 4 inches and $1/8$ inch thick. Cut out the small five-petal blossoms.

14. Add texture to the blossoms using a knitting needle or flower press. Place the flowers in egg molds to dry.

TO FINISH THE CAKE

15. Cover the cakes with the remaining 6 pounds of white fondant using the method on p. 22, and dowel and stack the cakes according to the directions on p. 26.

16. Gather all of the elements you've made and have them ready to apply as you decorate the cake. Decorate the cake the same day you plan to serve it.

17. Create the branches by hand-rolling the remaining $1/2$ pound of white fondant into long, bumpy ropes that range in length from 2 to 8 inches. Hands are really the best tool for this job—the bumps in the rope help make them look like real branches.

VARIATIONS

The finish is monochromatic, so why not play with that idea and change up the colors?

All one color: This same idea would be gorgeous in a rich chocolate brown or icy pale blue.

Splash of color: Pick one element—I think the flowers or butterflies would be most successful—and make it bright and bold. To keep the look clean, apply a bit of restraint and stick with one statement color.

18. Brush a thin line of water onto the cake where you'd like the branches to go. Gently apply the branches to the cake. Use the tip of the knitting needle to add texture to the branches.

19. Fill a small piping bag fitted with a #2 or #3 tip with royal icing. Often, I use a small spatula when applying royal icing to glue on decorations. This cake design has so many pieces, however, so you'll save yourself time by using a piping bag.

20. Decide where you want the flowers to go—along the branches or at the ends of the branches. Pipe a small dot of icing onto the bottom tip of each petal before you place it. The points of the petal should all face the center to create an open flower. To finish the flower, pipe a small bead of royal icing in the middle of it. Place a pea-sized ball of fondant in the center of the flower. Use the tip of the knitting needle to add texture to the flower center. Continue until you have placed all of your flowers. Place the buds and smaller flowers along the branches.

21. When placing the leaves, place them alongside the branches or the flowers. You can get creative when placing the butterflies. Channel your inner Bob Ross—and add a bit of artistic interpretation. Maybe a little butterfly lives on top of the cake; place a few little leaves here or there. There are no mistakes in nature, only happy accidents.

22. Place the completed cake in a cool, dry place until ready to serve—your fridge might be too humid, and that could cause the cake's molded elements to soften. This design is best done the day the cake will be served.

SMALLER SHINDIGS

Scale down the size of this cake to meet the needs of your event.

- The cake would look beautiful as a small two-tiered cake or even as a single cake. If you create a single cake, concentrate your decor on the top, as opposed to the sides, since that will be the focal point of the cake.
- The elements would also make a simple but dramatic cupcake display. Create the leaves, flowers, butterflies, and buds and use them to adorn cupcakes baked in silver wrappers and topped with white frosting. Arrange them on platters or cake stands to create an edible porcelain garden.

MAKE *it* BETTER

Use the same fondant to cover the cakes as well as make the design elements. This will keep the color uniform.

Topiary Cake & Cupcakes

PERFECT FOR A SPRING BABY SHOWER OR BRIDAL SHOWER—OR EVEN A GARDEN-THEMED birthday party—this cake is great for a crowd with mixed tastes. You can create the cake bites that make up the topiary top in one flavor or a few different ones and the flower pot cake in yet another flavor. Enhance the design by adding fondant flowers to the cake bites, and use them to help your guests differentiate between the various flavors.

FOR THE WOODEN BASE

10-inch round wooden or Masonite cake base

Drill

$1/2$-inch × 12-inch wooden dowel

One 2-inch-long flat-top wood screw

FOR THE CAKE AND CUPCAKES

8-inch round cake, not crumb-coated (filling optional)

1 pound Vanilla Swiss Meringue Buttercream (see p. 198)

$1/2$ pound brown fondant, $1/2$ pound orange fondant, and 2 pounds ivory fondant OR 3 pounds ivory fondant and gel food colors in orange and brown

2 cups melted chocolate ganache (see p. 200)

2 cups crushed chocolate cookies or chocolate cake crumbs

14 ounces brown candy melts

14 ounces green candy melts

Approximately 60 cake bites, uncoated

Green sprinkles, single color or color mix

Cake-Making Tools (p. 10)

6-inch Styrofoam ball

Fork or slotted spoon

Toothpicks

Parchment-paper-lined sheet pan

TO MAKE THE WOODEN BASE

NOTE: *Securing the dowel, which creates the "stem" of your topiary, to the cake base will give your cake an added layer of security. The wooden base can be reused each time you make this cake.*

1. Using a ruler or tape measure, find the center of your wooden cake base and mark it with a pencil.

2. Predrill the center of your cake base and the end of your dowel so that the screw will easily fit into it. Place the pre-drilled dowel end over the hole in the cake board and screw the pieces together from the bottom up using a flat-topped screw.

TO MAKE THE FLOWER POT

NOTE: *For a flower pot with untapered edges, crumb-coat the 8-inch round cake with Vanilla Swiss Meringue Buttercream and skip to Step 4.*

1. To taper the edges of your cake, place the 8-inch round cake on a turntable. You'll be working on the cake as if the flower pot is sitting upside down, with the smaller part toward the top and larger opening toward the bottom. Filling the flower pot base is optional, but if you decide to do so, chill it for at least 2 hours (or until firm) before tapering it. When filled, the flower pot base should be 4 to 5 inches tall.

2. Cut a circle that's $6^{1}/2$ inches in diameter out of parchment paper. Center the parchment paper circle on top of the cake. Hold the circle down, and use the serrated knife to slowly carve the cake away, working from the edge of the parchment paper circle diagonally out to the bottom edge of the cake. Stand in one place and turn the turntable as you work to trim all of the edges.

continued

3. Gently turn the cake over. It should resemble the shape of a terra-cotta pot. Trim away any areas that seem lopsided or a little off. Crumb-coat and chill it for 1 hour, or until firm.

4. Spread 3 to 4 tablespoons of the buttercream on the wooden cake base near the dowel. Use a ruler to find the center of the bottom of your flower pot cake. Align the top of the dowel with the center bottom of the cake, and carefully slide it down the dowel until it sits on the cake board.

5. If you are working with precolored fondants, knead the brown, orange, and ivory fondant together to get a terra-cotta color. If you are dyeing fondant, start with 3 pounds of an ivory color as your base and mix in a pea-sized amount of brown gel food color and a slightly larger pea-sized amount of orange gel food color. Color intensity can vary based on the manufacturer, so once your initial colors are mixed, add more brown if your fondant seems too light or more orange if your fondant seems too brown.

6. The best way to cover the flower pot cake is by using the pieced fondant technique on p. 24. Roll out about $2^1/2$ pounds of the terra-cotta-colored fondant until it's about $1/4$ inch thick and wrap the side of the cake with fondant. Leave the top of the cake uncovered. To create the flower pot lip, roll out the remaining terra-cotta-colored fondant to create a ribbon that is 28 inches long by $1^1/2$ inches wide and $1/4$ inch thick. (For ribbon directions, see p. 39.)

7. Brush a little water on to the top $1^1/2$ inches of the flower pot. Roll the fondant ribbon up like a spool and apply the ribbon to the flower pot's top edge, starting at the cake's seam and unrolling and pressing all the way around. Trim away any excess fondant where the seams meet. Fill the seam using the method described on p. 24.

8. To give the top of the pot a clean, sharp edge, cut a hole in the center of a 10-inch cake board and lightly place it on top of the cake. Hold the board down lightly with one hand and use the other hand to gently press the ribbon upward so that it meets the board. When you remove the board, you should have an even top edge.

9. Spread most of the chocolate ganache on top of the cake inside the flower pot rim, and sprinkle it with most of the ground chocolate cookies (or cake) to create the effect of potting soil. Next, carefully cover the exposed cake board at the base of the cake with a light layer of the remaining ganache, and sprinkle it with the remaining "dirt."

TO DECORATE THE CAKE BITES

10. Melt the brown candy melts according to the package instructions. Paint the entire dowel with the melted candy and push the Styrofoam ball onto the top. The melts will act like glue to keep the ball in place and help the dowel look more like a tree trunk.

11. Melt the green candy melts in a medium-sized microwave-safe bowl and paint the entire Styrofoam ball with it. Don't use all of the melted candy; you'll need some for covering the cake bites. Work on the cake bites while the foam ball dries.

12. Drop the cake bites, one at a time, into the bowl of melted green candy melts. Using a fork or slotted spoon, roll the bite around until it is completely coated.

13. Remove the coated cake bite with the fork or slotted spoon and, while the coating is wet, roll it in a shallow dish filled with green sprinkles. Place the coated cake bites on a parchment-lined sheet pan to dry. Repeat for each cake bite until all are coated. It's okay if your bites set with a little footed edge for this project—that will be the side you press against the topiary base.

PUT IT TOGETHER

14. Place a wooden toothpick into the very top center of the green Styrofoam ball. (Toothpicks are ideal because they won't add weight to the cake.)

15. Press a cake bite onto the toothpick so the flat edge of the cake bite is against the ball. It's easier to start with the toothpick in the ball, rather than the toothpick in the bite. Work your way down around the ball, filling in as much space with cake bites as you can.

16. Once your topiary is assembled you can leave it as is or decorate it with fondant flowers, butterflies, or bees—anything found in a garden. Apply these finishing touches by dipping the end of a toothpick into the melted green candy coating. Place a small dot of coating where you want the decoration to go and gently press the decoration onto the dot until set.

MAKE IT *or* FAKE IT!

You can get the same look for the top of the topiary using any round chocolate candy (like Ferroro Rocher®). Finish the candy the way you would the bites by rolling it in the melts and sprinkles. If you're short on time, top cupcakes with store-bought, flower-shaped lollipops.

4

Graphic Designs

BOLD, CRISP LINES AND BRIGHT COLORS HELP BRING THE MODERN

designs in this chapter to life. As in an art museum, a clean backdrop allows

a graphic design to "pop." When creating graphic designs, think less about

the intricate details and focus more on the outlines of shapes. The fewer

details you use to create an image, the more modern it will appear.

Make it Pretty Basics

Here are some tips that will help you with the cakes in this chapter.

- All of the cakes in this book are made up of four cake layers (baked in two pans and split in half), unless otherwise instructed.

- Use a brush of water to adhere fondant. Heavier pieces may require using piping gel, buttercream, or royal icing.

- In warmer months, working in an air-conditioned room is best. Finished cakes should be stored in the fridge overnight, or at room temperature if being served that day.

Stained Glass

CREATING SOPHISTICATED BIRTHDAY CAKES IS ALWAYS A DIFFICULT TASK. FOR THIS cake, I gathered inspiration from the stained glass windows found in modern American architecture. The base is made up of three cakes, which gives it the height necessary to create an airy design that complements the tighter design on the top tier. When the time comes for you to design a cake for your family or friends, try to see beyond their likes and dislikes. Think about what inspires them, what they find beautiful, and what makes them happy.

FOR THE CAKE

One 6-inch square cake and three 8-inch square cakes, filled and crumb-coated (see pp. 14–15; pp. 18–19)

5 pounds white fondant

Approximately 2 pounds black fondant

1/4 to 1/2 pound each red, yellow, blue, and green fondant

Cake-Making Tools (p. 10)

Small paintbrush

3-inch, 1-inch, and 1/2-inch round cutters

1/2-inch square cutters (or you can cut squares using a knife)

Piping gel

NOTE: *This design takes longer to explain than to do. The essential rule is to apply the shapes in the right order: Outline the cake's edges, apply the circles, outline the circles, apply the interior lines, apply the colored squares, and then outline the squares. Adding the circles first makes it easier to create sharp lines coming out from a circle's rounded edges. Circles are much more difficult to work into a design that's already laid out square.*

TO OUTLINE THE FRONT OF THE CAKE

1. Cover the cakes with white fondant using the method on p. 22, and dowel and stack the cakes according to the directions on p. 26.

2. When decorating this cake, it's best to work from the edges in. Start by rolling the black fondant until it's 1/8 inch thick. Use a ruler and sharp knife to cut the fondant into 1/4-inch-wide strips that are 5 to 6 inches long for the top tier and 8 to 9 inches long for the bottom tier. They will be used to outline your cake, so you want them to be a little longer than the longest edge of your cake.

NOTE: *If you have to join two strips together to create a seam, use the seam-filling techniques on p. 24.*

3. Beginning on the top tier, brush a thin line of water along the front top edge of the cake. Pick up a cut strip from both ends and apply it where you just applied the water. Guide the line straight with a ruler before it sets into place. Use a knife to

continued

SMALLER SHINDIGS

- Cut the fondant shapes used in the design and trim their edges with a thin line of black fondant. Allow the shapes to dry out for at least an hour (ideally, overnight) and use them to top cupcakes.
- To create a similar patterned look to that of the cake, roll out white fondant and place the colored fondant shapes and black strips directly onto the fondant while it's flat on the table. Use round or square cutters to cut out pieces of the pattern and use them as cupcake toppers.

trim the edges of the black line flat at the corners of the cake. Repeat on the bottom front edge of the same cake, and again on the top and bottom edges of the bottom tier.

4. Next, outline the sides of the cake, applying the black fondant strips as you did in Step 3. Use a knife to trim the black side strips so they meet the strips on the top and bottom of the cake without overlapping.

TO APPLY THE CIRCLES

5. Roll out the yellow fondant until it's $1/8$ inch thick and cut out one 3-inch and one 2-inch circle. Brush a small amount of water onto the back of the 3-inch circle, and apply it to the upper left corner of the top tier. Leave about $1/2$ inch between the edges of the cake and the circle. Apply the smaller circle to the bottom left corner of the bottom tier in the same way, but leave about $1\frac{1}{2}$ inches between the edges of the cake and the circle; see Figure 1.

6. Roll out the red fondant until it's $1/8$ inch thick, and cut out one 3-inch circle. Brush a little water onto the back of the circle and apply it to the lower right corner of the top tier. Leave about $1/2$ inch between the edges of the cake and the circle. Repeat the step again using the blue fondant and cutting a 1-inch circle to place about $1/2$ inch from the upper right corner of the top tier, see Figure 1.

7. After all the circles have been placed, roll a portion of the remaining black fondant and cut it into strips that are 6 to 8 inches long and about $1/4$ inch wide. Brush the edges of the circles with a little water and use these strips to outline the circles.

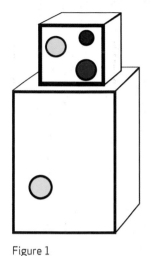

Figure 1

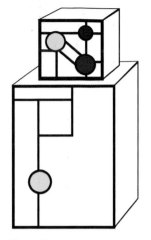

Figure 2

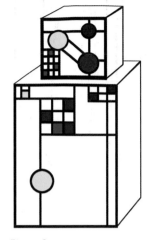

Figure 3

TO APPLY THE STRIPS AND SQUARES

8. When applying the strips that run from the edge of a circle toward the edge of the cake, you can be creative with your placement. Use the black lines to create boxes on the cake as shown in Figure 2.

9. Once you've formed a general outline with your strips, set the black fondant aside and roll out a colored fondant to $1/8$ inch thick. Cut two to four $1/2$-inch squares; repeat with other colors. (I used four green squares, three red squares, two blue squares, and one yellow square.)

10. Working within an outlined space on the cake, place the colored squares to create a grid, leaving about $1/8$ inch of white space between some of the squares; see Figure 3.

11. Roll out the remaining black fondant so that it's $1/8$ inch thick. Cut about fifteen $1/4$-inch-wide by 2-inch-long strips and apply them to create a grid over the colored squares. The strips should connect the edges and interior black lines on the cake. It's okay if these strips overlap within the cake design; see Figure 3.

12. Once the design is fixed in place, brush a small amount of piping gel onto the colored shapes only. This gives them a bit of shine against the white matte fondant and adds to the glassy feel of the design.

MAKE IT *or* FAKE IT!

Trimming thin fondant strips can be time-consuming, so if you're looking for a quicker fix, try using black rope licorice instead. No colored fondant? No problem. Grab a box of fruit leather and cut your stained glass shapes from it.

Pierrot

THIS IS ONE OF THOSE STYLES OF CAKE THAT INSTANTLY IMPRESSES. WHILE THE TIERS look like they're perilously perched on top of one another, the cake is actually quite secure. Topsy-turvy cakes are a little more time-consuming to make than a standard stacked cake. For this reason, I really like to use this design when it matches well with the theme. The queen of hearts, carnivals, and clowns (of course) are all excellent sources of inspiration here. Bright colors are an obvious choice for this kind of cake, but this design is striking in its use of black and white with touches of silver.

FOR STACKING THE CAKE

Two 6-inch, 8-inch, and 10-inch round cakes, not filled or crumb-coated

4 pounds white fondant

2 pounds black fondant

20 cups buttercream

Cake-Making Tools (p. 10)

FOR DECORATING THE CAKE

3 pounds black fondant

3 pounds white fondant

One 4-ounce container 4-mm edible silver pearls

One 4-gram container of silver luster dust

3-inch round cutter

1/4-inch round cutter

2-inch-tall diamond-shaped cutter

Piping gel

Small bowl with a lid (or small plastic storage container)

Vodka or any clear extract

Small paintbrush

See p. 91 for cupcake supplies.

TO CUT AND STACK THE CAKE

1. Adhere one 10-inch round cake to the cake board using a dab of buttercream. Use a long serrated knife to level the top of the cake (see p. 14). Discard the cake top. Then cut the cake in half horizontally at the center so you have two equal portions (see Figure 1 on p. 88). Set the cake aside.

2. Place the other uncut 10-inch round cake on the turntable. Level the top of the cake, and discard the cake top.

3. Slice the cake in half diagonally from the upper right edge of the cake to the bottom of the opposite side. Do not spin the cake! Hold it still and move only the knife. Remove the top portion of cake, and turn it so that both fat ends are on the same side—this is what creates the diagonal top of your cake (see Figure 1 on p. 88). Set this cake aside.

4. Return to the first 10-inch cake and fill it as you normally would. Then, cover the top with buttercream and place the bottom half of the second 10-inch cake on top of it. Apply a thinner layer of buttercream to the top of this layer and apply the next cake, keeping the fat sides together. You should now clearly see the sloping top of the bottom tier of the topsy-turvy cake (see Figure 2 on p. 88).

5. For the 8-inch middle tier, cut the diagonal on the top cake so that it isn't quite as steep: Start from the upper right edge of the cake and cut to the middle of the opposite side. Fill as in Step 4.

continued

6. For the 6-inch top tier, follow Steps 1 through 4.

7. Once you've filled all of the tiers, crumb-coat them and allow them to chill until they're completely firm, about 3 hours. Now you're ready to stack them.

8. Center an 8-inch round pan on top of the 10-inch tier. Use a small knife to trace the circle of the pan onto the center of the cake. Following the line you just traced, use a serrated knife to cut a wedge out of the taller side of the top layer of your bottom tier (as shown in Figure 3). Remove the wedge of cake that you just cut. You should now see the flat surface where the next tier of cake will be placed.

9. Cover the 6-inch and 10-inch tiers with white fondant according to the directions on p. 22. After the fondant has been secured to the top of the 10-inch tier, cut away the fondant that's covering the indentation in the center of the cake. Cover the middle tier with black fondant. Dowel the layers according to the directions on p. 26 before stacking them. When you place the middle tier, its base should fit snugly into the flat circular space you created on the tier below. Stack the top tier on the middle tier just as you would stack a traditional cake. When stacking, place the higher ends of each tier to be opposite each other when you stack them.

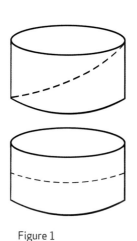

Figure 1

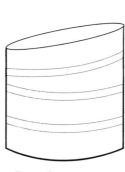

Figure 2

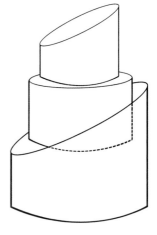

Figure 3

TO DECORATE THE CAKE

1. Roll out a quarter of the black fondant into a rectangle that's about 6 inches long by 8 inches wide and $1/8$ inch thick. Use the 3-inch round cutter to create three large fondant puffs according to the instructions on p. 38. Set them aside.

NOTE: *Allow the puffs to dry for at least 4 hours—ideally, overnight. They will be applied to the cake last.*

2. Roll out a quarter of the black fondant into a rectangle that's about 6 inches long by 8 inches wide and $1/8$ inch thick. Cut about 15 circles with the $1/4$-inch round cutter. You may need one or two more or less, depending on the height of your cake. These will be the polka dots on the top tier.

3. Place the circles around the bottom edge of the top tier, spaced about $3^1/2$ inches apart. Brush a bit of water on the back of the circle to adhere it to the cake. Apply the next row so that the circles are above but between the previously placed circles. When applying the third row, trim the circles as they run over the edges of the top of the cake. This helps keep the illusion of a repeating pattern as the shape of the cake changes. Apply the fourth row to the taller side of your cake in the same way.

4. For the center tier, roll out a third of the white fondant into a rectangle that's $4^1/2$ inches long by 32 inches wide and $1/8$ inch thick. Use an accordion cutter or a sharp knife and a ruler to cut this into three long strips that are $1^1/2$ inches wide each.

5. Start at the top of the middle tier and brush a small amount of water about $1/4$ inch down from the top edge of the cake. Roll up the white strip in a spool and unroll it onto the cake where you just applied the water. Use the edge of a ruler to gently guide the line straight.

6. Apply the other two strips to the tier and leave a $1/2$-inch space between each one. At the bottom of the tier, trim the edge of the strips where they meet the top of the cake in the tier below. This edge will later be covered by the white ruffle.

7. For the bottom tier you will need 60 to 70 diamonds, so work in small batches to keep them from drying out. Roll out a quarter of the black fondant at a time into rectangles that are about 8 inches long by 6 inches wide and $1/8$ inch thick. Cut out the diamond shapes.

continued

MAKE *it* BETTER

If your luster dust is too thin, wait! Let evaporation take away some of the liquid. Vodka evaporates quickly, so keep it on hand while working, just in case the luster dust paint starts to thicken.

8. To apply the diamond shapes, start at the tallest part of the bottom tier. Place the first diamond so that the point touches the top edge of the cake. Place the next diamond below it so that the top point of that diamond touches the bottom point of the diamond above. Place a third diamond in the same way below the second diamond. Trim the third diamond where it meets the bottom edge of the cake. Start your next row of diamonds, making sure the points on the sides of the diamonds touch the points of the diamonds from the first row. As you work your way around the cake, trim the diamonds at the top and bottom edges of the cake so that they don't reach over the edge.

9. Use piping gel to apply edible silver pearls at the points where the diamonds touch.

10. To finish the bottom tier, create the ruffle using the technique on p. 42. Apply the ruffle around the top edge of the bottom tier. The ruffle is made up of many pieces, so work with strips that are $1/2$ inch wide by 3 to 4 inches long. Apply the ruffles to the cake by brushing on a bit of water or piping gel. Place the ruffles right up against each other to give the illusion of one long ruffle.

11. In a small bowl, mix a few drops of vodka or clear extract with the silver luster dust. Start with a tiny amount of liquid—just a few drops—until the luster dust has the consistency of acrylic paint. You don't want it as thin as watercolor.

12. Use a small paintbrush to apply the silver luster paint to the edges of the ruffle. If you're not happy with the coverage after the first coat, allow it to dry and then apply a second coat.

13. To finish the cake, use piping gel to apply the three large black puffs in a row on the top and middle tiers.

NOTE: *This cake design is best created shortly before the cake will be served. If you plan to work on it ahead of time and store it in the fridge, wait to apply the puffs until you're ready to serve the cake. Without the puffs, the cake can be refrigerated overnight. Once the puffs have been applied, keep the cake in a cool, dry place until ready to serve.*

Pierrot Cupcake

TOPSY-TURVY CAKES DON'T JUST REQUIRE A LOT OF TIME; THEY ALSO END UP PROVIDING a lot of servings. For a smaller party (and a similar look without the carving), create a topsy-turvy cupcake stack.

FOR THE CUPCAKES

12 mini cupcakes baked in white wrappers

12 standard-sized cupcakes baked in black wrappers

12 giant cupcakes baked in white wrappers

2 cups Swiss meringue buttercream

1 container black sprinkles

One 4-ounce container 2-mm edible white pearls

12 black mini fondant puffs (see p. 38)

TO CREATE THE STACK

1. Frost each of the cupcakes with Swiss meringue buttercream (cream cheese frosting is too soft for this).

2. To stack the cupcakes, first place a standard cupcake on top of a giant cupcake so that it's a little tilted to one side. Next, place a mini cupcake on top of the standard cupcake, but tilt it in the opposite direction. Top with sprinkles and edible pearls.

3. Add a fondant puff to the front of each cupcake, and you have a supercute, small topsy-turvy cake.

4. Once all of the cupcakes are completed, refrigerate them for at least 20 minutes to allow the buttercream to set. They may also be refrigerated overnight, but take them out about 30 minutes before serving to allow them to come to room temperature.

Sweet Shoppe

SUGAR AND SPICE AND EVERYTHING NICE, THAT'S WHAT THIS CAKE IS MADE OF! THIS IS the perfect cake for baby showers, because it can be made in pink or blue. If the baby's gender is a surprise, make the candy swirls in any combination of the mommy-to-be's favorite colors or in shades of yellow or pale green. Not just for baby showers, this design would also work well on a "candy and sweets" table at a wedding or at a birthday party. Keep the pastels—or swap them for bright primary colors. Add a "1," and it's a sweet first birthday cake, too.

FOR THE CAKE

6-inch, 8-inch, and 10-inch round cakes, filled and crumb-coated (see pp. 14–15; pp. 18–19)

7 pounds ivory fondant

1 pound each dark pink and light pink fondant

$1/2$ cup buttercream

Extruder (optional)

Cake-Making Tools (p. 10)

Parchment-paper-lined cookie sheet

$1/4$-inch round cutter

Small paintbrush

FOR THE MINI CAKE

Six 3-inch round mini cakes, crumb-coated (see Mini Cakes on p. 16)

3 pounds ivory fondant

$1/2$ pound each dark pink and light pink fondant

TO MAKE THE CANDY SWIRLS

NOTE: *The swirls can be made up to a week ahead to save time when assembling the cake. Store them in an airtight container in a dark, dry place.*

1. Start with a piece of ivory fondant that's about the size of a golf ball. With both hands, roll the ball against a tabletop to create a rope. The rope should be about $1/4$ inch in diameter. (You could also use a fondant extruder for this, if you have one.) Repeat with one of the shades of pink.

2. Twist both ropes together to form a long, swirled rope. Pinch the rope at both ends to secure.

3. Start at one end and coil the rope up to create a swirled disk. Secure the end of the rope to the swirl with a bit of water.

4. Lay the fondant swirl flat on a table and lightly roll a plastic rolling pin over the top of the swirl to smooth the surface. It doesn't have to be completely smooth—it just helps give the appearance of an old-fashioned rolled lollipop.

5. Repeat this technique with both shades of pink fondant, using ropes of varying lengths to create larger and smaller swirls. You should have nine swirls for each shade of pink: three small, three medium, and three large. Place the swirls on a parchment-paper-lined cookie sheet to dry overnight or for at least 12 hours. They must dry completely to keep their shape.

continued

TO MAKE AND APPLY THE CANDY DOTS

1. Cover the cakes with 6 pounds of the ivory fondant using the method on p. 22, and dowel and stack them according to the directions on p. 26.

2. Roll out the remaining lighter pink fondant into a small rectangle that's $1/4$ inch thick. Cut out sixteen $1/4$-inch circles.

3. Adhere the circles to the bottom tier of the cake using a little water brushed on the back of the circles. Start with one vertical row, and place the first circle about $1/4$ inch from the bottom edge of the cake. As you work, hold a ruler vertically against the cake to help you keep the line straight. Place the next circle a little less than an inch above the first one, and work your way up the tier until you have four circles in a vertical line. Repeat to create three more lines that are spaced a little less than an inch apart.

4. Once the four rows of the light pink circles have been applied, run your fingertip around the edges of each circle to soften the hard line created by the cutter. This helps give the appearance of the paper dot candy that inspired this design.

5. Repeat the dot-making Steps 2 through 4 with the remaining dark pink fondant.

6. Alternate from light to dark circles after every four rows until you've gone all the way around the bottom tier of the cake.

FINISHING THE CAKE

7. Apply the candy swirls in a cascading pattern to the top and middle tiers of the cake. Use a small dab of buttercream to secure each swirl to the cake. Use the larger swirls on the middle tier and work your way up to place smaller swirls on the top tier. This is a fun, whimsical look, so feel free to apply the swirls in whatever way you think looks best.

TO MAKE THE MINI CAKES

NOTE: *For an impressive individual dessert, create candy swirl mini cakes (see Mini Cakes on p. 16). Or for a creative take-home treat, wrap the mini cakes in clear cellophane and tie the ends with pink curling ribbons. Trim and fluff the cellophane ends so that your mini cake looks like a giant piece of candy!*

1. Cover the mini cakes in ivory fondant according to the directions on p. 22.

2. Roll out a golf-ball-sized piece of pink fondant (either shade) into a rectangle that's 6 inches long by 1 inch wide and $1/8$ inch thick. It should be large enough to cut two ribbons from it.

3. Cut each ribbon diagonally to create four long triangular strips. Use these strips to create the larger stripes on your mini cake. Apply the strips, one at a time, by placing the point of the triangle in the middle of the cake and laying the strip down over the side of the mini cake and slightly curving it around the side. Trim away any excess fondant from the bottom.

4. To create the thinner strips, start with a similar amount of fondant in the other shade of pink.

5. Roll out the fondant into a rectangle that's about 6 inches long by $1/4$ inch wide and about $1/8$ inch thick. Cut four ribbons from it.

6. Trim one end of each of the strips so that it forms a point.

7. Apply the strips to the mini cake in the same way you applied the thicker ones, placing a thinner strip in between each of the thicker strips. Repeat for all six mini cakes.

8. Store the mini cakes in the refrigerator in an air-tight container for up to 3 days. Allow the mini cakes to come to room temperature before serving.

MAKE IT *or* FAKE IT!

Use real candy if pressed for time. For the dots on the bottom tier, use candy-coated chocolates. The candy swirls can be done with real lollipops that have had their sticks trimmed away. Or make swirls using different kinds of bendable candy like licorice ropes or taffy. Apply real candy to your cake just as you would apply any fondant decoration. You can skip the fondant finish and apply candy directly to a buttercream-finished cake. Rustic or piped pearl buttercream finishes would work well.

Rainbow Hearts

IN SIXTH GRADE, MY DEAREST POSSESSIONS WERE MY STICKER BOOK, MY CAT, AND MY rainbow hearts sweatshirt (I'm a child of the '80s). Little did I know at the time that my sweatshirt would become the inspiration for one of my most popular cake designs. This cake is a pure celebration of love, happiness, and color. It makes a funky, fun wedding cake or a cheerful birthday cake. In fact, I'd have this cake anytime.

FOR THE CAKE

6-inch, 8-inch, and 10-inch round cakes, filled and crumb-coated (pp. 14–15; pp. 18–19)

6 pounds white fondant

1 pound each red, orange, yellow, green, light blue, lavender, and pink fondant

Heart cookie cutter, $1^1/2$ by $1^1/2$ inches

Plastic wrap

Masking tape

$3/8$-inch-wide ribbon (to use as a spacer)

Cake-Making Tools (p. 10)

Small paintbrush

SMALLER SHINDIGS

The fondant hearts on this cake are fantastic cupcake toppers. If time allows, let the hearts dry firm so that they can be applied standing up a bit.

- Bake the cupcakes in black or white wrappers, which allows the color hearts to really pop.
- Arrange the cupcakes in a rainbow pattern on a platter or jumbled up for a fun, casual look.

TO MAKE AND APPLY THE HEARTS

1. Cover the cakes with the white fondant using the method on p. 22, and dowel and stack them according to the directions on p. 26.

2. Roll out the red fondant to $1/8$ inch thick. Cut out fondant hearts and cover them with plastic wrap to keep them from drying out. Repeat the process for all the fondant colors. You will need to make 36 hearts for the top tier, 48 hearts for the middle tier, and 60 hearts for the bottom tier. It's best to work in small batches so the fondant doesn't dry out.

3. To apply the hearts, decide where the front of the cake will be. Use a small piece of masking tape to mark that spot on the cake board. This is important because you will always start placing hearts at the front of the cake.

4. Brush the back of a red heart with a little water and apply it to the bottom center of the top tier. (I suggest starting with red, since it's first in rainbow order.)

5. Work from the center front to the center back, placing the hearts so that they touch at their thickest part. Working to the right of the red heart, apply an orange heart. To the left of the red heart, working in reverse rainbow order, apply a pink one. Working from both sides of the first heart helps keep the design clean on the front of the cake, since by the time the line meets in the back, you may end up with two similar colors next to each other.

6. Once the first row is complete, use two small pieces of masking tape to gently hold the $3/8$-inch ribbon in place around

continued

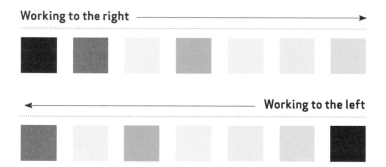

Variations

This design is very versatile.
For a Valentine's design:
Create the hearts in shades of pink and red. The same hearts could be used as cupcake toppers with sweetheart messages written on them using edible markers.
For a different look: Use the same method, but change the hearts to rounds, stars, or whatever matches your theme. Or you can create ombre color patterns by using the same color in various shades.

the cake above the first row of hearts. The bottom of the ribbon should be right up against the tops of the hearts. This becomes a spacer and offers a straight edge against which to line up the next row of hearts.

7. Start the next row by placing a pink heart in the center above the first red heart. Above the orange heart, apply a red heart, and so on. Following this pattern gives the illusion of the colors wrapping up the sides of the cake. Remove the spacer ribbon, and use it again for the next row.

8. Repeat these steps for all three tiers of the cake. Always begin with the bottom row of hearts and work your way up.

Heart color chart

To keep organized and move quickly, write down the heart color order for quick reference while decorating or refer to this chart when decorating. Place the red heart first, and work to the right of the cake in rainbow order. When working to the left of the red heart, work in reverse rainbow order.

Working to the right ⟶

Working to the left ⟵

MAKE IT *or* FAKE IT!

Fruit leather is my go-to product for creating brightly colored designs in a hurry. The colors available in supermarket brands may not complete a rainbow, but they can still be used to make a bright and cheery pattern on a cake.

Alphabet Cake

THIS ALPHABET CAKE IS SO SIMPLE, AND THE LETTERS ARE INSTANTLY RECOGNIZABLE as the plastic A, B, C fridge magnets kids love. (I do believe they are a requirement in any house with children in it.) While precious as a first birthday cake, it really works for any age birthday—just spell out the child's age or name on it.

If you're going for a random letter pattern, keep an eye out for mystery words! You don't want to unintentionally spell something unflattering on your child's cake. So while you're decorating, take a step back and see if any of your random letters aren't as random as they should be. Your choice: Make the letters from fondant or candy melts.

FOR THE CAKE

6-inch and 8-inch square cakes, filled and crumb-coated (pp. 14–15; pp. 18–19)

4^1/$_2$ pounds white fondant

Cake-Making Tools (p. 10)

Small paintbrush

Piping gel

FOR THE FONDANT LETTERS

^{1}/$_4$ to ^{1}/$_2$ pound each of bright color fondants for letters (four to five colors)

Parchment-paper-lined cookie sheet

Alphabet cookie cutters

FOR THE CANDY LETTERS

1 cup each brightly colored candy melts

Small microwave-safe bowls and spoons for melting candy

Alphabet candy mold

Offset spatula

TO MAKE AND APPLY THE FONDANT LETTERS

1. Cover the cakes with white fondant using the method on p. 22, and dowel and stack them according to the directions on p. 26.

2. Use a plastic rolling pin to roll out one of the pieces of colored fondant to ^{1}/$_4$ to ^{1}/$_2$ inch thickness. Refrigerator letter magnets are thick, so mimic that depth to achieve a realistic look. Cut out letters from the rolled fondant, and place them on a cookie sheet lined with parchment paper to dry overnight or at least 3 to 4 hours. Repeat this step with the other colors. Allowing them to dry is important so they hold their shape when applied.

3. Once the letters are firm, apply them to the cake as you desire. Brush a small amount of water or piping gel onto the back of the letter before you apply it to hold it in place.

continued

TO MAKE AND APPLY THE CANDY LETTERS

1. Cover the cakes with white fondant using the method on p. 22, and dowel and stack them according to the directions on p. 26.

2. Place one of the candy melt colors in a microwave-safe bowl and heat in 15- to 25-second intervals. Stir between every interval to keep the candy melts from burning or clumping. Brands can vary, so be sure to read the manufacturer's melting instructions.

3. Once it's smooth, pour the melted candy into the alphabet mold. Don't rush, but work quickly before the candy starts to set. Run the offset spatula over the top of the mold to remove any excess candy melt. Gently tap the mold against the tabletop to disperse any air bubbles that might have formed.

4. Let the candy melt molds set until firm, about 20 minutes, depending on the temperature of your room. Speed up the process by popping them into the fridge for 10 minutes. Once they're firm to the touch, unmold the letters and repeat with the other colors.

5. Depending on the size and thickness of your candy letters, they may stick to the fondant with just a brush of water. If they are bit heavier, use piping gel to keep them in place.

SMALLER SHINDIGS

Either of the letter methods from this project works great as cupcake toppers.

Bake cupcakes in brightly colored wrappers and mix and match letters for a fun look. Or use the letter-topped cupcakes to spell out a happy birthday message.

MAKE IT *or* FAKE IT!

Cookie letters work well for this cake if you're in a pinch! You can buy them premade. To add color, melt a small amount of candy melts and dip the front of the cookie in it. Allow it to dry, and use the color-dipped letters to decorate a buttercream-finished cake or use them as cupcake toppers. If you use the cookies on a fondant-finished cake, affix them with a small dab of buttercream.

Floral Creations

FLOWERS ARE A MAINSTAY IN CAKE DESIGN, AND FOR GOOD REASON.

They provide an endless source of inspiration—from the shapes of their petals to the variety of colors found in just one bloom. The flowers in this chapter range from crafty stamped appliqués and simple fondant blossoms to more complex blooms made of wired gum paste petals.

Make It Pretty Basics

Here are some tips that will help you with the cakes in this chapter.

- All of the cakes in this book are made up of four cake layers (baked in two pans and split in half), unless otherwise instructed.

- Use a brush of water to adhere fondant. Heavier pieces may require using piping gel, butter-cream, or royal icing.

- In warmer months, working in an air-conditioned room is best. Finished cakes should be stored in the fridge overnight, or at room temperature if being served that day.

Craft Cake

SOMETIMES A CLIENT WILL ASK ME TO EXPLAIN A SPECIFIC KIND OF CAKE SKILL OR technique. Then almost immediately they'll say, "Never mind! I'm not an artist, and I could never do that." Well, you don't need to be an artist to decorate a cake. Templates, molds, and stamps provide foolproof ways to create new patterns and designs that are specific to your special event. Use a similar (but not the same) stamp to create invitations or other paper good details. If you want the pattern on your cake to match exactly, then I recommend purchasing two of the same stamp and keeping one in the kitchen and the other in the craft room.

FOR THE CAKE

1 pound gum paste

Gel food colors in black, pink, green, purple, and yellow

6-inch, 8-inch, and 10-inch round cakes, filled and crumb-coated (see pp. 14–15; pp. 18–19)

6 pounds white fondant

1 cup Swiss meringue buttercream

Small bowls for food color

Foam craft brush

Large flower stamp, washed and dried

Cake-Making Tools (p. 10)

Parchment-paper-lined cookie sheet

Small and medium leaf stamps

6-inch and 8-inch round cake pans

Fine-tipped paintbrush

Small metal spatula

TO MAKE THE STAMPED FLOWER APPLIQUÉS

NOTE: *The stamped flower appliqués can be made ahead to save time when assembling the cake. Store them in an airtight container in a dark, dry place. Stamped designs are sensitive to heat and humidity.*

1. Roll out the gum paste to about $1/8$ inch thick.

2. Pour a quarter-sized dollop of black gel food color into a small bowl. Dip a foam craft brush into it, gently wiping away any excess onto the lip of the bowl. Apply the gel food color to the stamp. Press the stamp gently and evenly onto the gum paste.

3. Repeat the stamping process to create four more black flower appliqués, reapplying the color to the stamp each time. If the stamp starts to accumulate food coloring, rinse it under warm water and dry it thoroughly before starting to stamp again.

4. Next, use a sharp knife or scalpel to cut around the stamped flowers, about $1/4$ inch from the outer line of the flower.

5. Move the stamped appliqués to a parchment-paper-lined cookie sheet, and allow them to dry thoroughly overnight.

6. Repeat the same technique using the leaf stamps to create five leaf appliqués of each size.

continued

To create hand-stamped toppers for cupcakes, use the same appliqué process as described in this design but use a smaller flower stamp.

If a larger stamp is all you have, create the stamped pattern on a piece of white fondant. Paint in some areas with color and leave others black and white. Use a 3-inch round cutter and cut out areas of the stamped pattern to use as cupcake toppers.

Bake your cupcakes in black wrappers (to match the black outlines) or use complementary colored wrappers. Frost the cupcakes with white buttercream to complete the look.

TO DECORATE THE CAKE

1. Cover the cakes in white fondant according to the instructions on p. 22. Dowel the cakes according to the directions on p. 26, but do not stack them yet. Leaving the cakes unstacked will make them easier to stamp.

2. Stamp the cake using the same coloring and stamping process as for the appliqués. Start with the bottom tier and press the stamp onto the surface of the cake while applying gentle, steady pressure. Press firmly enough so that the stamp is even, but not so hard that the lines become blurred. Practice on the back of the cake or the cake top center, which will be covered by the other cakes when stacked.

3. When you have had enough practice, stamp the sides of the 10-inch cake with the flower stamp. Apply color to the stamp each time you use it. After creating the desired pattern on the cake, set the bottom tier aside.

4. Place an 8-inch round cake pan upside down in the center of the turntable and put the 8-inch round cake on top of that. Elevating the cake will give the clearance needed to bring the stamped design all the way down to the edges of the cake.

5. Repeat the stamping process. Set the cake aside to allow the gel color to dry.

6. Turn the 6-inch cake pan upside down on the turntable and put the 6-inch cake on top of that. Repeat the stamping process.

7. Once the stamped pattern is dry, stack the cakes according to the instructions on p. 26.

8. Use a fine-tipped paintbrush and black gel food color to fill in any broken lines or areas where the stamp may not have come all the way through. You could also use a black food-color marker for this. Set the cake aside until the gel color completely dries, 10 to 15 minutes.

9. To paint the stamped appliqués, pour a quarter-sized amount of each gel color into its own bowl. Use your smallest paintbrush to fill in the yellow centers of the flowers. Even though the black gel color is dry, avoid going over the black lines as much as possible so you don't smear the stamp. Paint the flower petals pink and purple, and paint the leaves green. Let the color dry for 10 to 15 minutes.

10. To apply the leaf and flower appliqués to the cake, spread a small amount of buttercream on the back of the appliqué using a small metal spatula. Place it on the front of the cake. I like to put two together on the top tier, with two more equally spaced apart on the second tier, and one on the bottom tier under the top tier of roses. You can place them wherever you feel they work in your design.

NOTE: *This cake holds up best when assembled the day it's served. It should be kept in an air-conditioned room, since the design is sensitive to humidity and heat.*

PAINTING TIPS

- When adding color, try not to paint over the black lines. Moisture from the gel food color can sometimes cause the lines to smudge.
- Try not to load the brush with too much paint; it's easier to add more paint than to take it away.
- Start in the center of the area being painted and brush out toward the black outline.

MAKE IT *or* FAKE IT!

If you don't have a stamp but want to create a fabulous stamped design, use vegetables. Yes, you read it right! Cut a potato in half and create your own stamp by carving a simple shape into it with a small sharp knife. For a faster fix, grab a bunch of celery (one that's still connected at the base). Cut the celery stalks about 2 inches from the base. The base is the perfect nature-made stamp: It creates the shape of a rose.

Flower Bouquet

THIS CAKE IS PERFECT FOR BRIDAL SHOWERS AND OTHER SPRINGTIME EVENTS, LIKE Mother's Day. Customize the bouquet by making the flowers in her favorite colors, or change up the design for Valentine's Day and use only pink and red ribbon roses. After all, who wouldn't love this gift? It's flowers and dessert all in one!

FOR THE CAKE

1 pound bright pink fondant

3 pounds pale pink fondant

1 pound purple fondant

6-inch-diameter dome-shaped cake, crumb-coated (pp. 14–15; pp. 18–19); (filling optional)

2 standard-sized cupcakes, unfrosted

1 cup buttercream

2 pounds lime green fondant

1 pound each sage green and leaf green fondant

1 pound white or yellow fondant

Piping gel

2 parchment-paper-lined cookie sheets

2¹/₂-inch five-petal blossom cutter

1-inch butterfly cutter

Extruder (optional)

2-inch daisy cutter

1-inch leaf cutter

Accordion cutter (optional)

Cake-Making Tools (p. 10)

MAKE AHEAD FLOWERS AND BUTTERFLY

NOTE: *Making what you can in advance will save you time the day of the event. In this cake, everything but the mums can be made ahead. If you prefer to make all of the flowers the same day, cover the cake with fondant first so you can place the flowers as you make them.*

1. To make the ribbon roses, use the bright pink fondant and 1 pound of the pale pink fondant to make 20 large ribbon roses (10 of each color) and approximately 14 smaller ribbon roses (about 7 of each color) according to the directions on p. 41. The larger roses should be 3 inches in diameter, which means the ribbon should be approximately 6 inches long. The smaller ribbon roses should be about ¹/₂ to 1 inch in diameter, so the ribbon should be approximately 2 inches long.

2. Set them on a parchment-paper-lined cookie sheet to dry while you make the other flowers.

3. To make the lisianthus, roll the purple fondant a little thicker than ¹/₈ inch thick. Cut 12 flower shapes using the five-petal blossom cutter.

4. Use a small sharp knife to cut a slit between two of the petals. The slit should reach down to the center of the blossom.

5. Start at one of the cut ends and roll up the flower. Start off with a tighter roll that becomes more relaxed toward the other cut end.

6. Trim the pointed end flat so that the flower will sit nicely on the cake.

7. Dry the flowers on a parchment-paper-lined cookie sheet.

continued

8. To make the butterfly, roll out a grape-sized amount of pale pink fondant until it's a little more than $1/8$ inch thick.

9. Cut out a butterfly and bend it slightly at the center.

10. Place the butterfly on a parchment-paper-lined cookie sheet with one wing up against a side, so that when the butterfly dries, its wings will be standing up and open.

TO DECORATE THE CAKE

1. Roll out 2 pounds of the pale pink fondant until it's $1/4$ inch thick, and cover the dome-shaped cake (see p. 22).

2. Create the stem bunch for the bouquet by placing two unwrapped cupcakes on their sides, bottom to bottom. Trim one side of both cupcakes so they lay flat on the cake plate. Use a small amount of buttercream to stick the cupcake bottoms together.

3. Place the top of one cupcake up against the side of the cake. Use buttercream to secure the cupcake to the cake and cake board.

4. Crumb-coat the cupcakes and chill the cake for an hour or so until firm.

5. Roll out $1/2$ pound of the lime green fondant until it's approximately 8 inches long by 5 inches wide and $1/4$ inch thick. Cover the cupcake stem bunch with the fondant and trim it to remove the excess.

6. To make the individual stems to place on top of the stem bunch, use your hands (or an extruder) to roll pencil-sized ropes from the sage green fondant, leaf green fondant, and remaining lime green fondant. You will need approximately 20 ropes.

7. Brush the stem bunch with a small amount of water, and apply the green ropes in random color order. Trim the ropes at the edge of the stem bunch. Continue until the stem bunch is entirely covered.

8. To apply the roses, brush a small amount of water or piping gel to the dome-shaped surface of the cake. Start by placing the large ribbon roses, so that the smaller, fluffier flowers can be placed in around them.

9. Next, place the smaller ribbon roses randomly on the surface of the cake, the same way you applied the larger ones. These smaller roses mimic tea or spray roses, which are tiny and come on branches with clusters of three to four roses per stem. Cluster your small ribbon roses when placing them on your cake for a similar effect.

10. To apply the lisianthus, use a small amount of water or piping gel to randomly adhere them in a few of the open spots left around the cake.

11. To make the mums, roll out a golf-ball-sized amount of the white (or yellow) fondant until it's a little thicker than $1/8$ inch. Cut out flower shapes using the daisy cutter.

12. Pick up the cut flower and use your fingers to pinch together the base of the flower while bringing the petals in toward each other. Trim the bottom flat so the flower can sit well on the cake.

13. To apply the mums, use water or piping gel to adhere the mums in the remaining open spaces. Spread the petals to fill out the space.

14. Fill in little gaps with green leaves. To do so, roll out a golf-ball-sized amount of green fondant (any green will do) until it's a little thicker than $1/8$ inch. Cut out about 30 leaf shapes.

15. Pinch and bend the leaves to fit them into the small open spaces. Tuck them in to cover any gaps between flowers.

16. Add a fondant ribbon to the stems. Roll out a golf-ball-sized amount of light pink fondant until it's $1/8$ inch thick. Use a sharp knife or accordion cutter to cut three strips that are 4 inches long by 1 inch wide.

17. Apply the strips over the middle of the fondant stems in a crisscross fashion and trim the ribbons at the cake board to give the illusion of ribbon-wrapped bouquet stems.

18. Finish the bouquet cake by perching the little pink butterfly on one of the large ribbon roses. Use a dab of piping gel to hold it in place.

MAKE IT *or* FAKE IT!

No time for fondant flower work? You can pick up premade fondant flowers at any cake decorating supply store. Most large craft stores now carry premade flowers as well.

The Graduate

WITH AN UPDATED TAKE ON THE CLASSIC TWISTED PARTY STREAMERS AND TISSUE PAPER puffs, this cake is an elegant addition to any graduation celebration. The pennant can be personalized with a name, initial, or celebratory message by using food-color markers. This design would also work well at a child's birthday party by changing the colors to match the party theme. Or use it as engagement party cake for a couple that met in school. The streamers and puffs could be done in their school's colors, and their initials or wedding date can be written on the pennant.

FOR THE CAKE

2 pounds burgundy fondant

2 pounds gold or mustard colored fondant

6-inch and 8-inch round cakes, filled and crumb-coated (pp. 14–15; pp. 18–19)

3$1/2$ pounds ivory fondant

$1/2$ cup buttercream for applying puffs

1 wooden lollipop stick

Parchment-paper-lined cookie sheet

Accordion cutter or sharp knife and metal ruler

Cake-Making Tools (p. 10)

MAKE AHEAD PENNANT AND PUFFS

NOTE: *The fondant pennant and puffs should be made the day before the event (or even earlier) and stored in an airtight container. This will give them enough time to dry before being applied to the cake.*

1. To make the pennant, roll out a golf-ball-sized piece of burgundy fondant to a rectangle about 5 inches long by 2 inches wide and $1/8$ inch thick. Cut a 4-inch by 1-inch strip from it.

2. Lay the strip horizontally, and place the wooden lollipop stick in the center of it. Fold the strip in half over the stick, and press the two sides of fondant together. Use a sharp knife to trim the edges of the strip to create the triangular shape of the pennant. Set the pennant aside on a parchment-paper-lined cookie sheet to dry.

3. To create the puffs in burgundy and gold, use the puff technique described on p. 38. For the top tier, you'll need to create six puffs (three of each color); for the bottom tier, you will need eight puffs (four of each color). Allow the puffs to dry completely before applying them to the cake.

continued

TO DECORATE THE CAKE

1. Cover the cakes with ivory fondant using the method on p. 22, and dowel and stack them according to the directions on p. 26.

2. Because the streamers need to be applied before they harden, make them in small batches. Roll out a golf-ball-sized piece of burgundy fondant into a strip that is about 5 inches long by $1/2$ inch wide and $1/8$ inch thick. Set that piece aside, and roll a similar size piece of gold fondant in the same way.

3. Lay the gold fondant on top of the burgundy fondant and use a rolling pin to lightly press the pieces together. Apply enough pressure so that the pieces stick together, but not so much that the colors start to blend.

4. Use a sharp knife and a metal ruler or an accordion cutter to cut a 5-inch-long by $1/4$-inch-wide strip from the layered piece of fondant.

5. Pick up the strip with both hands to gently twist it as you would a paper streamer, so both colors can be seen equally. Set it aside momentarily.

6. Brush two small spots of water, about 3 inches apart, on the top edge of the top tier of cake. Press the ends of the fondant streamer where you've brushed the water, and allow the streamer to hang off the cake in between. Repeat this process to create and place six streamers around the top tier and eight streamers around the bottom tier.

7. To arrange the puffs on the cake, place a small dab of buttercream onto the back of a puff. Gently press the puff into place where the two streamers meet. Repeat and alternate the puff colors as you continue around the cake.

8. To finish the cake, center and place the fondant pennant on top.

Ribbon Rose Hobnail

THIS CAKE WAS INSPIRED BY VINTAGE HOBNAIL GLASS AND THE SOFT, SNUGGLY, NUBBY chenille blankets that can be found tucked into a newborn's crib. Done in pale blue to welcome a baby boy, this cake would look just as precious in any pastel. Pinks, purples, yellows—even sage green would work. Use deeper or brighter colors and this would double as a sweet birthday cake for a girl of any age.

FOR THE CAKE

6-inch and 8-inch round cakes, filled and crumb-coated (see pp. 14–15; pp. 18–19)

$4^1/_2$ pounds white fondant

2 pounds pale blue fondant

2 ounces leaf green fondant

One 4-ounce container of 6-mm edible white pearls

$3^1/_2$-inch round cutter

Cake-Making Tools (p. 10)

Extruder (optional)

Small paintbrush

Parchment-paper-lined cookie sheet

MAKE AHEAD RIBBON

1. The ribbons for this bow should be 6 inches long by 3 inches wide (follow the ribbon technique on p. 39). To make the bow, use the bow technique on p. 40. Help the bow keep its shape by inserting a parchment paper tube into each ribbon loop to let the loops dry open. Allow the bow to dry for at least a day.

TO DECORATE THE CAKE

1. Cover the cakes with $3^1/_2$ pounds of white fondant using the method on p. 22, and dowel and stack them according to the directions on p. 26.

2. Roll out the pale blue fondant until it's 26 inches long by 3 inches wide and $^1/_4$ inch thick. It should be long enough to wrap around the bottom tier. You can cut shorter strips and fill in the seams (see the instructions for pieced fondant on p. 24), if you prefer.

3. Create a scalloped edge on one side of the pale blue strip by placing the $3^1/_2$-inch cutter half on the edge of the strip and half off—in other words, the fondant edge bisects the circle. Once the first semicircle is cut, begin the next one at its edge, creating a peak between each half circle.

4. Roll up the strip like a spool and unroll it around the bottom of the cake. Brush the cake with a small amount of water to help it adhere, if necessary. The seam will be covered later with a row of pearls.

5. Roll about $^1/_4$ pound of white fondant into a rope that's $^1/_4$ inch in diameter and about 26 inches long. You can use

continued

your hands or an extruder. Brush a small amount of water onto the cake along the scalloped edge of the blue ribbon and apply the rope. Start at the seam on the blue ribbon (this is so both seams match), and gently press the rope into place along the scalloped line.

6. To make tiny ribbon roses, pinch off a marble-sized piece of blue fondant from the remaining fondant and roll tiny ropes (about the size of a piece of yarn). Coil the roses as shown in the ribbon rose technique on p. 41. Try to keep the ribbon roses about the same size as the pearls. Set the roses aside on a parchment-paper-lined cookie sheet until you're ready to place them on the cake.

7. To make the tiny leaves for behind the ribbon roses, pinch off a very small amount of green fondant—about half the size of the ribbon rose. Use your fingers to roll the little bit of fondant into a teardrop shape. Press the teardrop between your fingers to flatten it into a leaf shape. Place the leaves alongside the ribbon roses on the cookie sheet and set aside to dry.

8. To create the pearl and rose pattern on the cake, start on the bottom tier and place a pearl or a rose onto the cake about $1/4$ inch above each scallop peak. Brush on a small amount of water or piping gel to help the pearl or rose adhere. If you are applying a rose, place the leaf with the rounded end under the rose, allowing the pointed end to stick out from behind it.

9. Next place a pearl or a rose about $1/4$ inch above the middle of each scallop. Use these two lines that you've created as a guide to apply the pearls and roses up the rest of the cake and space them about $1^1/2$ inches apart.

NOTE: *To create the pattern, use more pearls than roses. Place roses after every one or two pearls. Try to space the roses out evenly around the cake.*

10. To finish the design, brush a thin line of water around the bottom edge of the cake and line the edge with pearls. Brush the seam of the blue ribbon and cover it with pearls, too. Then top the cake with your blue bow.

Flower Lattice

LATTICE DESIGNS ARE NOT NEW IN THE CAKE WORLD. TAKE A LOOK IN CAKE DECORATING books from decades ago, and you'll find intricately piped lattices covering towering white confections. I put a decidedly modern spin on this design by using an infusion of bright green and a lattice that's reminiscent of the kind you'd find outside covered in flowering vines. Finishing the cake with intricately created, lifelike gum paste flowers adds to the overall elegance of the cake. Gum paste flowers are so beautiful and such works of art on their own that I like to keep the other design elements fairly simple. Keeping the lattice very clean and sharp allows the flower work to really shine as the center of attention. This cake is perfectly suited to a garden wedding or shower. It would also be a pretty addition to an early afternoon birthday or bridal tea.

FOR THE CAKE

$^1/_2$ pound gum paste

Fuchsia, lilac, and forest green petal dust

6-inch, 8-inch, and 10-inch square cakes, filled and crumb-coated (pp. 14–15; pp. 18–19)

8 pounds lime green fondant

2 pounds white fondant

Cake-Making Tools (p. 10)

CelBoard

Flower-Making Tools (p. 32)

Clematis leaf cutter

Lettuce leaf silicone press

120 premade flower stamens with orange or yellow tips (found in craft or cake supply stores)

Piece of Styrofoam, foam egg crate, or drying rack

Small paintbrushes

Steamer (or pot of boiling water)

Gum paste glue

Sweet pea cutter set (or template on p. 121)

Classic leaf silicone press

TO MAKE CLEMATIS FLOWERS

NOTE: *Clematis flowers can be made ahead and stored in a dry, dark place. They are made using the wired petal method found on p. 50.*

1. Roll out about $^1/_2$ ounce of gum paste over the grooves of a CelBoard until it is paper thin. Use the clematis cutter to cut out five petals. Thin the edges with the ball tool, and use floral wire to wire each petal. Repeat this step so that you have 25 wired petals—enough to make five clematis flowers.

2. Gently press the petals using the lettuce leaf press, and lay them in an egg tray to dry. When placing each petal into the egg tray, gently lay the petals into the rounded area of the tray so that they are slightly curved. If you create too deep a curve, the flower won't look "open" once the petals are all wired together. Allow the petals to set overnight so they are firm and dry before wiring.

3. To create the flower center, gather a dozen flower stamens and use floral tape to attach the stamens to floral wire. Repeat to create four more flower centers.

4. When the wired flower petals have dried, gently bend back the petal where the base of the petal meets the wire to form

continued

a nearly 90-degree angle. Arrange the five wired petals evenly around the flower center and secure them with floral tape. Make four more wired clematis.

NOTE: *With experience you'll be able to wire multiple petals at once, but if you're just learning how to work with floral tape, you may want to wire the petals together one at a time.*

5. Set the completed flowers aside by pushing the stem into a piece of Styrofoam or setting each flower gently on its side on a piece of foam egg crate.

6. To tint the clematis, brush the fuchsia petal dust over both sides of each petal.

7. To give the dusted flowers a pretty sheen and to keep the color from rubbing off, set the color using steam. If you have a steamer, hold it 6 to 10 inches away from the flowers so that the steam is just touching the petals. If you don't have a steamer, you can hold the flowers over a pot of boiling water— but don't let them touch the water. Steam each flower for only a few seconds. The petals will appear glossy once the color is set. Oversteaming the flower will make the color run and can cause the petals to wilt.

8. Place the steamed flowers back in the Styrofoam until needed. Protected from moisture and light, gum paste flowers will last for months. Create them when you have the time and keep them on hand for future use.

TO MAKE THE SWEET PEAS

NOTE: *Sweet peas are very loose and frilly flowers, so while there is a method to applying the petals, allow each one to fall a little differently. The less uniform the sweet peas are, the more realistic they will appear. They can be made ahead and stored in a dry, dark place. Make them using the glued petal method found on p. 48.*

1. Use tweezers to bend one tip of the floral wire to form a small hook, about 1/4 inch from the top.

2. Pinch off a pea-sized piece of gum paste and roll it between your fingertips to create a thin teardrop shape that is about an inch long.

continued

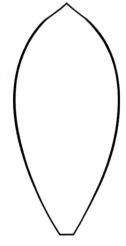

Clematis petal cutter template

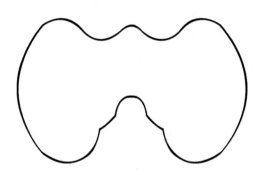

Sweet pea inner petal template

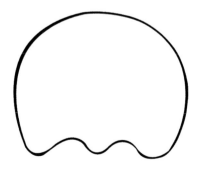

Sweet pea outer petal template

3. Dip the hooked end of the floral wire into the gum paste glue and then insert it into the thin end of the teardrop. Use your fingers to gently press the teardrop onto the floral wire. It should look something like a long, thin cotton swab.

4. Push the wire into a piece of Styrofoam, or bend it to hang dry on a rack. Allow the center to dry overnight before applying other petals.

5. Roll the gum paste paper-thin. (It should be thin enough to almost see through it, but not so thin that it falls apart.)

6. Use the sweet pea inner petal cutter or the template on p. 121 to cut a butterfly-shaped petal, and place it on a foam floral mat. Using the small end of the ball tool, apply firm pressure and roll the ball over the edges of the petal so that they begin to frill. Do this for every edge of the petal.

7. Apply a small amount of gum paste glue to the center of the petal (if it were a butterfly, where the body would be). Take one of the flower centers and place it in the center of the petal where the glue was brushed on. The top of the center should stick up a tiny bit over the edge of the petal. Bring the sides of the petal together up over the center, closing the petal around the center of the wire while leaving the outer edges ruffly. Place the flower aside in Styrofoam or on a rack to dry.

8. Repeat the sweet pea Steps 1 through 7 eight more times to create the other sweet pea flowers. Each flower doesn't have to be dried completely, but give it at least 30 minutes so the petal doesn't move when the next one is applied.

9. Roll the gum paste as thin as you did for the first petal, and use the sweat pea cutter that has more of an oval shape to cut nine more petals.

10. Place each petal on a floral foam mat and frill all of the edges with the ball tool. Brush a small strip of gum paste glue up the center of the petal from the little notch at the bottom of the petal to the top.

11. Pick up one of the flowers from the earlier petal step, and place the center onto the petal you just created. Bring the sides of the back petal together up and over the center in the same way, closing the back petal around the center petal, leaving the outer edges ruffly.

12. Stand the sweet pea upright in the Styrofoam or lay it on its side in the foam egg crate and let it dry overnight, until it's completely firm.

13. Use lilac petal dust to tint the sweat peas. Brush and steam them the same way you did for the clematis. Sweet peas have many different tones in each flower, so don't create a solid color. It's fine if some of the white gum paste shows through. That variation in color adds to the translucent feel of a real flower petal.

14. Stand the sweet peas in the Styrofoam again to dry, or lay them on their side on the foam egg crate. Once dry, they can be stored for later use.

TO MAKE THE LEAVES

NOTE: *Leaves can be made ahead and stored in a dry, dark place. They are created using the wired petal method on p. 50.*

1. Roll out $1/4$ pound of gum paste to $1/8$ inch thick. Cut out 10 leaves and wire each one. Press them in a classic leaf press to give them realistic leaf lines.

2. Lay the leaves flat or bend them slightly lengthwise through the middle and allow them to dry overnight. Make 9 leaves.

3. To tint the leaves, brush them with forest green petal dust and steam them to set the color. Set them aside to dry. Once dry, they can be stored for later use.

TO APPLY THE LATTICE

1. Cover the cakes with the lime green fondant using the method on p. 22, and dowel and stack the cakes according to the directions on p. 26. Use five dowels in the bottom tier and three dowels in the middle tier.

2. To make the lattice strips, roll out the white fondant to a rectangle that is about 12 inches long by 6 inches wide and $1/8$ inch thick to be sure you have strips long enough to run over the cake. Using a sharp knife and ruler, or an accordion cutter, cut the white fondant into 12-inch-long by 1-inch-wide strips.

3. Roll up a strip of white fondant into a spool. Place one end of the strip over the upper left corner of the top tier of the cake so

continued

This three-tier beauty can easily be scaled down to individual servings with a similar look.

- Create square mini cakes and top them with a single square of lattice.
- Place the lattice strips so that the points of the square are opposite the corners of the top of the mini cake.
- Top the cake with a single handmade gum paste flower, or decorate it with simpler fondant blossoms, like ribbon roses. In the mini cake shown on p. 123, I used three tiny five-petal fondant blossoms and a small green leaf.

that the point of the corner hits the strip in the center. Unroll the strip diagonally down across the side of the top tier to end in the middle of the bottom edge. Trim the strip at the top corner and bottom edge of the top tier. The first strip is the most important, because it will be the guide for the rest of the lattice.

4. To keep the lattice looking uniform, work in one direction at a time. Place the next strip about 2 inches to the right of the first strip on the same diagonal. Use a metal ruler to help guide the edges of the strip straight. Repeat the same process to add a strip to the bottom left side of the first strip.

5. With the first three strips done, it's time to work in the other direction. Repeat the same process, but start with the opposite top corner.

6. The process remains the same for all three tiers. Always start in the same corner and in the same direction so that your lattice appears uniform and clean. While the top tier requires three strips in each direction, the bottom two tiers will each need four strips in both directions.

TO APPLY THE FLOWERS AND LEAVES

NOTE: *For smaller flowers like sweet peas, creating a spray of a few flowers can be very pretty and also makes them easier to apply and remove. I've used a single sweet pea along side the two clematis on the top right corner of the first tier and another at the lower left corner of the first tier. I placed a spray of three sweet peas in the middle of the left hand edge on the second tier, and a spray of four at the top right corner of the bottom tier. But you can be creative when determining how many you want to use.*

1. Gather two or three sweet peas at the stems and arrange them in your hand so the flowers are at varying heights. Use floral tape to tape the stems together. Once the flowers are secured, add two or three leaves to the sides of the spray and secure them with floral tape.

2. To add the flowers to the cake, insert a plastic straw into the cake where the flowers will go. Cut the straw to match the length of the flowers' wires—you don't want the wires to touch the cake. Insert the straw into the cake where you want the flowers to go. Then arrange the wires of your flowers inside the straw. Placing the wires into the straw also makes it easy to remove the unit as a whole before slicing and serving the cake.

3. If you do not want to insert the flowers into the cake, you can use tweezers to gently coil the flower stem behind the flower. If the stem is too thick to curl, trim it very short behind the flower. Pipe a dollop of buttercream (or place a fondant ball where you want your flower to go) and insert your stem into that. Floral wires are obviously inedible, so be sure to let the person cutting the cake know to remove them before serving.

MAKE IT *or* FAKE IT!

Gum paste flowers of good quality can be purchased online from cake decorating supply sites. To customize premade gum paste flowers, buy them in white and tint them yourself so that the colors coordinate with your event and cake design. This design also lends itself to the use of fresh flowers—you can add them to your cake in the same way that you would apply gum paste flowers. Check with your florist on which flowers work best on cakes, and which can sit longest out of water.

Fabric, Bows & Buttons

FABRIC AND FONDANT ARE SO SIMILAR IN THE WAY THAT THEY move and fold that it makes sense that one would inspire the other! The fabric details explored in this chapter include pleats, ruffles, buttons, and bows. Dresses are an obvious source of inspiration, but also look to accessories, menswear, and linens to create unexpected details.

Make It Pretty Basics

Here are some tips that will help you with the cakes in this chapter.

- All of the cakes in this book are made up of four cake layers (baked in two pans and split in half), unless otherwise instructed.

- Use a brush of water to adhere fondant. Heavier pieces may require using piping gel, buttercream, or royal icing.

- In warmer months, working in an air-conditioned room is best. Finished cakes should be stored in the fridge overnight, or at room temperature if being served that day.

Vintage Fabric

INSPIRED BY A 1940s WEDDING THEME, THE CAKE'S PLEATS, MISMATCHED BUTTON CASCADE, and layered bow topper were created to reflect the bride's love of all things vintage. Although created for a wedding, this cake would work well for a bridal or baby shower.

FOR THE CAKE

1 pound each teal blue and coral fondant

Pearl luster dust

6-inch, 8-inch, and 10-inch round cakes, filled and crumb-coated (pp. 14–15; pp. 18–19)

8 pounds ivory fondant

4 pounds khaki-colored fondant

One 4-ounce container 6-mm edible ivory pearls (or handmade; see p. 147)

Cake-Making Tools (p. 10)

Various silicone button molds, ranging in size from 1/4 inch to 2 inches or round cutters ranging from 1/4 inch to 2 inches

Piping tip (#2 or #3)

Burlap or other fabric texture mat

Parchment-paper-lined cookie sheet

Small paintbrush

Piping bag filled with 1 cup buttercream

TO MAKE THE BUTTONS

NOTE: *Buttons can be made ahead and kept in an airtight container in a dry, dark place.*

1. If you are working with silicone button molds, follow the molding instructions on p. 44. Use about 1 pound each of coral and blue fondant to make approximately 25 buttons.

2. If you are working without molds, roll out the coral fondant to 1/4 inch thick, or as thick as you want your buttons to be. Gently press a texture mat onto the fondant with a rolling pin. Peel the mat away, and use the cutters to create buttons. Use the tip of a #1 or #2 piping tip as a cutter to make the button's holes. A knitting needle can be used to make even smaller holes or to add detail. Create the appearance of a lip around the edge of your buttons by gently pressing the next smallest size cutter onto your textured button. Create different shaped buttons by using various cutters like hearts, squares, diamonds, etc. For smooth buttons, repeat the same process but omit the texture mats.

3. With either technique, when the buttons have set, add shimmer by dry-brushing them with luster dust.

TO DECORATE THE CAKE

1. Cover the cakes with 6 pounds of ivory fondant using the method on p. 22, and dowel and stack the cakes according to the directions on p. 26.

2. Roll out 1 1/2 pounds of ivory fondant to a little more than 1/4 inch thick. Texture the fondant with a burlap or other fabric texture mat by placing the mat onto the fondant and gently

continued

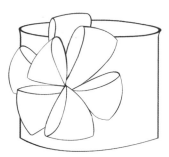

Figure 1

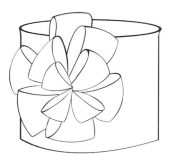

Figure 2

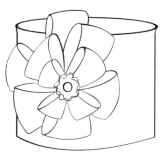

Figure 3

rolling over it with a rolling pin. Peel the mat away, and from the textured fondant, cut ribbons in the following dimensions:

- 2 ribbons that are 5 inches long by 2 inches wide
- 1 ribbon that is 4 inches long by 2 inches wide
- 2 ribbons that are 4 inches long by 1 inch wide
- 1 ribbon that is $1\frac{1}{2}$ inches long by 1 inch wide

3. Turn the ribbons into loops using the technique on p. 40. Place the loops on a parchment-paper-lined cookie sheet to set for 10 to 20 minutes. You will be using them while they are still soft and pliable, so make them on the same day you plan to decorate the cake. Lay them flat to dry—not open on their sides like a package bow.

4. Repeat the loop steps using the khaki fondant in the following dimensions:

- 1 ribbon that is 5 inches long by 2 inches wide
- 2 ribbons that are 4 inches long by 2 inches wide
- 2 ribbons that are 3 inches long by 1 inch wide

5. Pipe a dime-sized dab of buttercream at the base of one of the longest ivory loops; attach it on the side of the top cake tier so that it sticks up about an inch above the edge. Slide a small metal spatula inside the loop and use it to press the back of the loop to the cake. This helps to prevent squishing the texture pattern.

6. Apply one of the longest khaki loops to the left of the ivory one using the same technique. Layer it so that the tip of the khaki loop overlaps the tip of the ivory loop ever so slightly. The top of the khaki loop should sit a little lower than the top of the ivory loop. Place the next two ivory loops just below the first two loops in the same direction (see Figure 1).

7. Work in a circle to create a bow, and place a khaki loop to the right of the two ivory loops. Then place an ivory loop and a khaki loop, and end with an ivory loop (see Figure 2).

8. Add a quarter-sized amount of buttercream to the center of the bow where the ribbon loop tips meet to secure the next row of smaller loops; also continue to add a small amount of buttercream to the back of each loop before you apply it. In the center, place a smaller khaki loop facing out to the right; working in a half-circle, place the ivory loop next to it so the loop is facing down. Then place the final small khaki loop next to the ivory one (see Figure 2).

9. Roll out approximately 4 ounces (a golf-ball-sized amount) of ivory fondant so that it's $1/4$ inch thick. To finish the center of the loop, cut the fondant into $1/2$-inch-wide strips and create a ruffle according to the instructions on p. 42. There should be buttercream still exposed from applying the loops; use that to secure the ruffle. Use a ball tool to press the ruffle into the center of the bow. Pipe a tiny pearl of buttercream into the center of the ruffle, and finish it with one of the buttons.

10. Each pleat on the bottom tier is made from a single piece of fondant and should be rolled out one at a time. To make the pleats, start with a piece of khaki fondant that's about the size of a deck of cards. Roll the fondant to $1/8$ inch thick and cut from it a rectangle that's 5 inches long by 4 inches wide.

11. Bring each long side of the fondant rectangle toward the middle and curve it under, like a scroll, while keeping the side that's facing down flat. The edges of the rectangle should touch the inner edges of the fondant tube. There will be an open seam on the back side.

12. On the bottom tier, lightly brush a bit of water on the area where the first pleat will go. Place the pleat with the seam side against the cake and the flat side out. Press the center of the pleat against the cake, so that the top and bottom of the pleat retain the open shape. Insert the blade of a small metal spatula into the top opening of the pleat loop, and press it against the back seam to further secure the pleat to the cake.

13. Repeat the process around the cake, lining up each pleat edge so that it appears to be one large pleated piece of fabric.

14. To finish the bottom tier, roll out ivory fondant to $1/8$ inch thick. Use a sharp knife and a ruler (or an accordion cutter) to cut a $1/2$-inch-wide strip that is approximately 32 inches long. Apply the strip around the center of the pleated tier; secure it with water if needed.

15. Finish the cake with the buttons. Pipe a small pearl of buttercream onto the back of each button and then press them onto the cake so they cascade from the bow down to the ruffles at a diagonal. Add $1/2$-inch buttons to the ivory strip around the pleated tier. Place a few edible pearls between the cascading buttons to finish the design.

MAKE IT *or* FAKE IT!

Candy button cupcake toppers are quick and easy to create. Use round candies without a glossy finish (like Smarties® or Necco® wafers) and draw buttonhole dots in the center using a food-color marker. If you'd like, add swirly lines or stripes to embellish the candies.

SMALLER SHINDIGS

- For a vintage look on a smaller scale, add fondant buttons in different shapes and sizes to the tops of cupcakes.
- Or, for a show-stopping individual dessert, create small square mini cakes, and run a ruffle across the top. Finish with fondant ribbon and buttons for a look that's similar to the bottom tier.

Victorian Elegance

IF YOU HAVEN'T NOTICED, I LOVE A GOOD BOW. THEY'RE SIMPLE TO CREATE AND MAKE QUITE an impression. If left on my own, I'd probably put one on every cake! This cake design is a celebration of classic ribbons and bows. The frames and silhouette add a vintage Victorian feel. As is, this cake is a beautiful birthday cake for a teen (or younger) girl. Change the colors to a pastel palette, and it would fit right in at a baby shower.

FOR THE CAKE

6-inch and 10-inch round cakes, filled and crumb-coated (pp. 14–15; pp. 18–19)

Extra-tall 8-inch round cake, filled and crumb-coated

6½ pounds bright pink fondant

3 pounds black fondant

1 teaspoon old gold luster dust

Fine-tipped black food-color marker

1 pound white fondant

Vodka or clear extract

One 4-ounce container 6-mm edible black pearls (or handmade; see p. 147)

Cake-Making Tools (p. 10)

1-inch heart-shaped button mold

4-inch and 2-inch oval cutters

4-inch and 2-inch silicone frame molds

Extruder (optional)

TO DECORATE THE TOP TIER

1. For the extra-tall cake tier, bake one extra cake round. Cover the cakes with 6½ pounds of pink fondant using the method on p. 22. Dowel and stack them according to the directions on p. 26.

2. Roll out 1 pound of the black fondant large enough to cut a ribbon that's 19 inches long by 3 inches wide and 1/8 inch thick. Brush a small amount of water around the center of the top tier. Roll up the fondant ribbon into a spool, and pinch the exposed end so the corners are touching. Apply the pinched end to the center front of the top tier, and unroll the ribbon around the middle of the cake. Pinch the other end in the same way and press it onto the cake. Where the tapered ends meet is the front of the cake, and where the bow will be placed. Use a ruler to guide the ribbon straight if necessary.

3. Make a bow from ribbons that are 5 inches long and 3 inches wide using the technique on p. 40. Apply the bow directly to the cake on top of the tapered ends. The bow loops should lie fairly flat against the cake.

4. Mold a small heart-shaped button according to the directions on p. 129. If you don't have a mold, roll out black fondant to 1/8 inch thick and cut a heart shape using a 1-inch cutter. Run your finger along the edge of the cut heart to soften it.

5. Brush the heart with the luster dust. Apply the heart just below the center of the bow. Use a small amount of water to adhere it if needed. Use the food-color marker to draw a tiny black line between the heart and the bow center. This gives the illusion that the heart is a little charm hanging from the bow.

continued

TO DECORATE THE CENTER TIER

6. Roll out $1/2$ pound of black fondant to $1/8$ inch thick. Roll it large enough to cut two 5-inch-long by 2-inch-wide ribbons, and one 3-inch-long by 2-inch-wide ribbon.

7. Apply the shortest ribbon to the center front of the middle tier so that it starts at the base of the top tier and hangs over the top edge of the middle tier. Center it just below the bow and heart.

8. Apply the longer ribbons to the left and right sides of the middle ribbon about 2 inches away from it. Start at the base of the top tier and go down.

9. Make the frame centers by rolling out a quarter of the white fondant to $1/8$ inch thick, and cut one 4-inch oval and two 2-inch ovals. Apply the large oval so that it touches the edge of the center black ribbon. Apply the two smaller ovals so that they sit at the ends of the two black side ribbons.

10. If you are using silicone frame molds, create the frames using black fondant. For molding instructions, see p. 44. Make one large 4-inch-long frame for the center. Make two 2-inch-long side frames. Brush a thin layer of water onto the backs of the frames and apply them around the white ovals, overlapping the black ribbon.

11. If you are not using frame molds, make frames by rolling out black fondant to $1/4$ inch thick. Cut strips that are long enough to frame the ovals and no more than $1/8$ inch wide. Place them around the ovals. Create the top flourish of the frame by using an upside-down heart. Use a texture mat or a knitting needle to add details to the frame. Be as creative as you like.

12. Combine about $1/2$ tsp. luster dust with a few drops of vodka or clear extract to create a fluid paint. Brush the gold luster paint over the black frames, being careful not to get the gold onto the ivory or pink. Only paint on one thin layer of the gold paint to achieve a metallic patina.

NOTE: *If you get gold anywhere you don't want it, wipe the spot away using a cotton swab dipped in vodka.*

13. Roll a grape-sized amount of black fondant into a thin rope that is about the thickness of a piece of yarn (or use an extruder). Use the rope to create initials in the smaller frames. Or, write in the initials using a black food-color marker.

14. To finish the center frame, roll a golf-ball-sized amount of black fondant very thin, less than $1/8$ inch thick. Place the silhouette template (see sidebar at right) on top of the fondant to use as a guide. Cut out the silhouette using a scalpel or X-ACTO knife.

15. Handle the silhouette as little as possible once it's cut from the fondant so that it retains its shape. Brush a thin layer of water onto the center circle. Lift the silhouette using a small metal spatula. Gently apply the silhouette to the center of the middle frame.

16. To create two small bows to sit above each of the side frames, use the bow technique on p. 40 and ribbons that are 3 inches long and $1^{1}/_{2}$ inches wide. Apply the bows directly to the cake using a small amount of water if needed to decorate the bottom tier.

17. Roll the remaining black fondant into a rectangle that is $1/8$ inch thick and large enough to cut six 7-inch by 2-inch ribbons. Roll up the ribbon into a spool. Place it at the bottom edge of the middle tier and unroll it down to the edge of the bottom tier. Work your way around the cake, and space the ribbons about 3 inches apart.

18. Roll out the remaining white fondant into a rectangle that is $1/4$ inch thick and large enough to cut six ribbons that are 7 inches long by 1 inch wide. Roll up the ribbons into a spool and apply them centered between the black ribbons. Using the back of a knife or a knitting needle, score a line down the center of each white ribbon after it's been applied to the cake.

19. Following the bow technique on p. 40, create small black bows for the end of each of the black ribbons. Create the bow loops from ribbons that are $3^{1}/_{2}$ inches long and 2 inches wide.

20. To finish the cake, apply the pearls to the bottom edges of the top and middle tiers. (If you're making your own pearls rather than using premade, they should be about the size of a large pea.)

HOW TO MAKE A SILHOUETTE

Take a profile photo of the person you want to silhouette.

Print out the picture so that it's no more than 3 inches tall and 2 inches wide.

Use a black magic marker to fill in the silhouette. You'll use this as a guide from which to cut the fondant silhouette. Also, coloring in the picture first will give you a better idea of how your final silhouette will look and provide the opportunity to tweak it before cutting it out in fondant.

Once your silhouette is filled in, cut it out with a pair of scissors, and you have a template to use.

Toile

I LOVE A WEDDING GOWN WITH AN UNEXPECTED TWIST. THIS CAKE WAS INSPIRED BY A gorgeous white wedding gown that had an underskirt of pink toile. Tiny ribbons pulled the edges of the skirt up just a hint, so that when the bride walked there were little flashes of pink patterned fabric showing from underneath. This cake design can work well with any wedding theme—just change the color of the flowers or use a different pattern. It would also fit right in at an elegant bridal or baby shower tea.

FOR THE CAKE

8 pounds of white fondant

Pink petal dust

6-inch, 8-inch, and 10-inch round cakes, filled and crumb-coated (pp. 14–15; pp. 18–19)

Pink gel food color

Peony flower-making supplies (p. 50)

Cake-Making Tools (p. 10)

1-inch-wide ribbon (any color)

2 ball-headed pins

3-inch round cutter

Large floral stamp or printed image of a flower

Small paintbrush

TO MAKE THE FLOWER

1. A few days before making the cake, create a white peony topper using the peony technique on p. 50. Give it plenty of time to dry before use. Color the finished peony ever so slightly by dusting its center with pink petal dust.

TO DECORATE THE CAKE

1. Cover the cakes with 6 pounds of white fondant using the method on p. 22, and dowel and stack them according to the directions on p. 26.

2. Use a ruler to find the midpoint on the front and back sides of the middle tier, and mark it with a small pinhole. Connect the points by wrapping a piece of ribbon around the cake slightly above the center point and securing it to the cake on each side using ball-headed pins. (The pinholes will be covered later by fondant drapes and ribbons.)

3. With the ribbon as a guide, use the round cutter to mark half-circles around the cake. Don't make deep indentations; just mark the fondant ever so slightly. This will be your guide when applying the draping. Once the cake has been marked all the way around, remove the ribbon and pins.

4. If you are using a stamp, follow the technique on p. 105 to stamp the bottom half of the cake below the drape marks. Be careful not to stamp above those lines. If that happens, use a damp cloth to gently wipe away the stamped food color.

continued

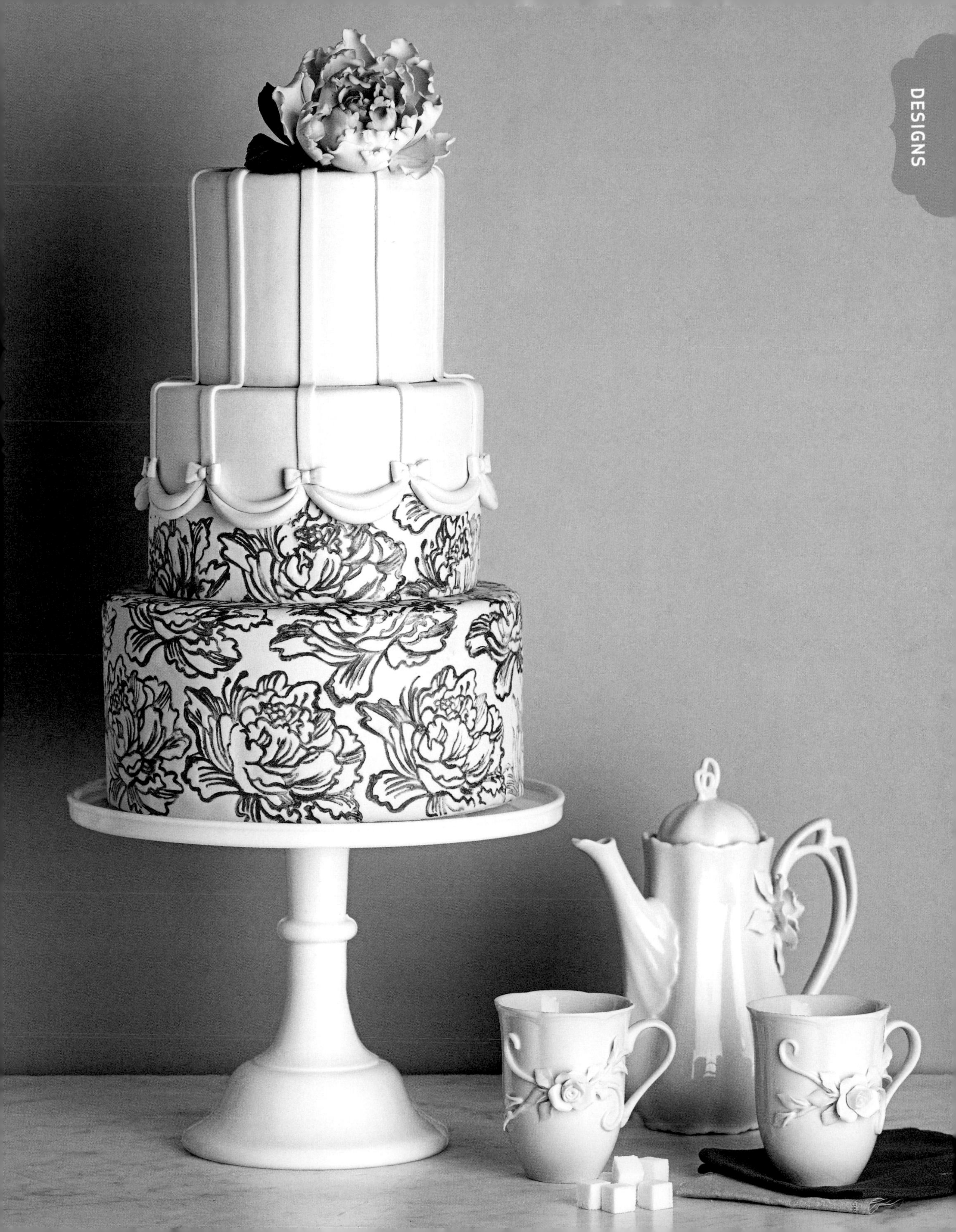

To create tea-party-worthy cupcake toppers, use the same technique to stamp or paint a pattern on a flat piece of fondant.

- Use round cutters to cut away cupcake-topper-sized disks. Allow the disks to dry before placing them on the cupcakes.
- The tiny bows from this cake would also make adorable toppers on cupcakes that were baked in pink wrappers and frosted with white buttercream.

5. If you are using a printed image of a flower, hold the image up against the side of the cake and trace the outline of the flower onto the fondant with a knitting needle. Apply firm but gentle pressure so that it marks the surface of the cake but doesn't pierce the paper or fondant. Do this around the tier, but be careful not to go above the drape line.

6. Trace over the lines with a paintbrush dipped in pink gel color.

NOTE: *Once the floral pattern is complete, create the ribbons before adding the draping so that the floral pattern has time to dry.*

7. Roll out half of the remaining white fondant to $^1/_8$ inch thick and follow the ribbon instructions on p. 39 to create ten strips that are 12 inches long by $^1/_4$ inch wide and $^1/_4$ inch thick.

8. Roll up the ribbon into a spool and place the end of it at the point where the two drapes will meet. Uncoil it up the side of the cake to the middle of the top tier. Press the ribbon so it lies flat against the side of the middle and top tier. If necessary, use a small amount of water to help it adhere and a metal ruler to gently guide the line straight. Unroll all the strips around the cake in the same manner, allowing the ends to overlap in the middle of the top tier.

9. To cut away the ends of the ribbons on top of the cake, press a 3-inch round cutter gently into the top of the cake, but not so hard that it goes through the layer of fondant covering the cake. Roll out a $^1/_4$-inch-thick piece of white fondant and cut out a 3-inch circle; place it on top of the cake to fill in where you trimmed the ribbon ends away.

10. Use the remaining white fondant to create the drapes following on the technique on p. 43. Start with a rectangle that is 4 inches long by 3 inches wide and $^1/_4$ inch thick. When completed, each drape should measure 3 inches from tip to tip when hanging and about $1^1/_2$ inches at its widest point.

11. Finish the cake by creating the tiny bows that sit in between each drape. Roll out the leftover white fondant, and follow the instructions for the bow technique on p. 40. The ribbon should be as thick as the ribbon already on the cake: $^1/_4$ inch wide by 1 inch long for each bow loop. The finished bows should be about an inch long.

12. Apply the bows to the cake by brushing on a small amount of water where each drape joins.

Ribbon Loop Cascade

I LOVE TO TAKE TRADITIONAL ELEMENTS AND USE THEM IN NEW WAYS. IN FLORAL ARRANGING, ribbon loops are sometimes attached to wires and inserted into bouquets. Cakes are commonly decorated with cascades of flowers, so I thought why not create a cascade of ribbon? This cake, done all in ivory, makes for a stunning, sculptural wedding cake. If desired, color could be subtly added to the ribbon loops in pale shades, or you can create an ombre effect by arranging the ribbon loops with the darker shades toward the bottom and lighter shades toward the top. To take the cake in a completely different direction, use brightly colored ribbon loops for a fun, present-inspired birthday cake.

FOR THE CAKE

9 pounds ivory fondant

6-inch, 8-inch, and 10-inch round cakes, filled and crumb-coated (pp. 14–15; pp. 18–19)

2 cups buttercream in a piping bag

Parchment-paper-lined cookie sheet

Cake-Making Tools (p. 10)

MAKE *it* BETTER

The cascade narrows as it moves toward the top of the cake, so the ribbon loops used at the bottom should be wider and longer than the thinner, shorter ones at the top.

MAKE THE LOOPS

NOTE: *Because this cake needs so many ribbon loops, it's best to make them in small batches so the fondant doesn't dry out. Loops can be made ahead and stored in an airtight container for up to a month. Loops that haven't properly dried will crack and crumble when pressed onto the sides of the cake.*

1. Make the loops in batches, rolling $1/2$ pound of the fondant at a time to a little more than $1/8$ inch thick. It will take about 3 pounds of fondant total.

2. Follow the ribbon loop technique for the bow tutorial on p. 40 to create loops that range in size from $1^1/2$ inches thick by 3 inches long (after being folded) to 1 inch wide by 1 inch thick (after being folded). For this design, trim the pointed ends of the ribbon loops flat. This will make it easier to attach them to the cake. You will need approximately 20–30 loops of each size.

3. As the loops are made, place them on a parchment-paper-lined cookie sheet to dry. Set them on their sides with the ribbon loop open. Allow the loops to dry for a few days—on a design like this one, it's easier to place the pieces when they are firm.

continued

TO DECORATE THE CAKE

1. Cover the cakes with the remaining 6 pounds of ivory fondant using the method on p. 22, and dowel and stack the cakes according to the directions on p. 26. Make sure your tiers are chilled all the way through (ideally overnight, or at least 3 hours) before decorating. This makes the loop-attaching process easier.

2. To attach the ribbon loops, pipe a pearl-sized amount of buttercream onto the tip of the loop and press the loop onto the right side of the bottom cake tier. Apply pressure on the tip of the loop only. Try not to apply pressure to the open part of the loop or it will break.

3. Work your way up the right side of the cake. Place the loops in different directions and use their natural shape to tuck them into each other.

SMALLER SHINDIGS

Creating drama on a large cake can take as many as a hundred ribbon loops. For drama on a smaller scale, just create a few ribbon loops and use them to fill the tops of cupcakes. Bake the cupcakes in white wrappers for a monochromatic look, or use brightly colored wrappers and bows for a cheery set of birthday cupcakes.

MAKE *it* BETTER

When creating a cascade of anything on a cake, start by making a thin triangle outline using the decorations as a guide. Then go back and add more to either side of the triangle to fill out the cascade. This does two things: It gives you a starting shape to work from so that the cascade doesn't go wonky, and it ensures that you won't run out of decorations. Starting with a smaller shape and adding to it helps you use the decorations more efficiently.

Gentleman's Cake

MOST CAKES (ESPECIALLY THE ONES I DESIGN) HAVE A DECIDEDLY FEMININE FEEL.
So I created this one for the gentlemen in our lives. The decorations are all inspired by menswear details—from the bow ties on top to the giant French-cuff bottom tier. For a more formal affair, switch out the brown and blue tones for black and white ones, and mimic the details of a tux.

FOR THE CAKE

6-inch, 8-inch, and 10-inch round cakes, filled and crumb-coated (pp. 14–15; pp. 18–19)

4 pounds ivory fondant

3 pounds brown fondant

4 pounds white fondant

2 pounds navy blue fondant

Bronze luster dust

1 tsp. vodka or clear extract

Burlap or tweed texture mat

Three textured mats (varying textures)

Cake-Making Tools (p. 10)

2-inch round cutter

$1^{1}/_{2}$-inch round cutter

Fine-tipped paintbrush

TO DECORATE THE CAKE

1. Cover the 6 inch cake using $1^{1}/_{2}$ pounds of the ivory fondant, the 8-inch cake using 2 pounds of the brown fondant, and the 10-inch cake using $2^{1}/_{2}$ pounds of the ivory fondant according to the directions on p. 22. Dowel and stack them according to the directions on p. 26.

TO TEXTURE THE MIDDLE TIER

2. While the brown fondant is still soft, align the edge of the burlap or tweed texture mat with the bottom edge of the middle cake tier. Use firm but gentle pressure to press the texture mat into the brown fondant. To keep the cake from sliding, place your other hand on the opposite side of the cake.

3. Peel the mat away from the fondant, move the mat to the right of the textured area, and line up the edge of the mat with the textured edge. Press the mat into the smooth fondant as you just did. Work around the cake until the side is textured.

NOTE: *The pattern should be consistent, so if the texture isn't as deep in some places, run back over that small spot with the mat. The lines don't have to be exact because these fabric patterns (like burlap or tweed) should have a random crosshatched look.*

continued

TO MAKE THE BOW TIES

NOTE: *Don't feel obligated to use my specific textures for each bow tie. The overall idea is to have three different colored bow ties with three different textures.*

4. Roll out the remaining pound of brown fondant large enough to cut a strip that's 19 inches long by 1 inch wide and $^1/_4$ inch thick; you should also have enough left over to cut another ribbon for the bow. Before cutting the strip, texture the fondant with a striped texture mat, or create freehand lines using a ball tool or knitting needle.

5. Roll up the brown strip into a spool and apply it around the cake just below the upper edge of the top tier. Apply the ribbon so the seam lands where you would like to place the bow tie. If necessary, brush on a small amount of water to help it adhere.

6. Make a bow tie from the same textured fondant following the bow technique from p. 40. To create the loops, use ribbons that are 2 inches wide and 5 inches long. Bow ties have a stiffer appearance than tied ribbon bows, so keep the lines sharp.

7. Apply the bow tie to the cake at the ribbon seam while the bow is still soft so that it lies flat against the cake. Do not apply the bow after it has dried, or it will stick out too far from the cake. To adhere it, brush on a small amount of water if needed. Slide a small knife or metal spatula in between the bow loops, and press the back of the bow against the cake to further secure it.

8. Create navy and white bow ties by following the technique described above, but use a dot texture mat for the navy bow and a thinner stripe mat for the white bow. I recommend making the white bow tie first and placing it along the bottom edge of the top tier before you create the navy one. Doing so allows you to center the navy bow tie between the brown and white bow ties. Stagger the bows so they are not on top of each other.

TO MAKE THE FRENCH CUFF

9. Roll out the remaining 3 pounds of white fondant to $^1/_4$ inch thick, in a size large enough to cut a 32-inch-long by 5-inch-wide strip. This is a very large piece of fondant to work with, so if you would rather, work with two 16-inch by 5-inch strips.

10. Roll up the fondant strip into a spool. Brush the sides of the bottom tier with a small amount of water to help adhere the white fondant cuff. Start the seam so it lines up with the navy bow on the top tier, and unroll the large white strip around the bottom tier. Keep the strip in line with the bottom edge of the cake, and unroll the white fondant all the way around the cake, allowing the white fondant to overlap where the strip started. Use a small sharp knife to trim away any excess white fondant so that it's even with the top of the tier.

NOTE: *If using two strips of white fondant, start with one piece and line up the edge with the navy blue bow tie. Unroll the piece of fondant so the seam lands on the back of the cake. Start your next strip where the first strip ends. Unroll across the front of the cake, slightly overlapping where you started. Use a small sharp knife to trim away any excess white fondant so that it's even with the top of the tier. Fill in the seam by following the instructions on p. 24.*

11. To create a rounded edge on the cuff, use the knife to cut away the top corner of the part of the fondant that overlaps the seam. Gently use the knife to pull away the overlap so that it sticks out from the side of the cake. Use your fingers to smooth the edge where you cut the corner away.

12. Roll out the remaining navy blue fondant to $1/4$ inch thick, long enough to cut four strips that are 32 inches long by $1/4$ inch wide. Again, it can be tricky to work with ribbons this long, so feel free to cut the strips in half.

13. Roll up one navy blue strip into a spool and apply it to the bottom tier about $3/4$ inch from the top edge. As you unroll the strip, pull the coiled ribbon away and toward the surface of the cake. Let the strip stick to the cake on its own instead of pushing it on with your fingers. Work your way down the tier, placing each strip $3/4$ inch away from the previous one. Use a metal ruler to help guide the lines straight as you apply the strips. I find that when applying horizontal lines, the less I handle the strips, the better.

NOTE: *If you are cutting the navy strips in half, start the strips so that the seams line up with the seam from the white strips. Fill in the seams according to the directions on p. 24.*

continued

TO MAKE THE CUFF LINK

14. Roll out the leftover brown fondant to $1/4$ inch thick, and cut out a 2-inch circle. Take the $1^1/2$-inch circle cutter and flip it over to the rolled edge and gently press it onto the cut round of fondant to create a ridge. Using the cutter upside down on its rolled edge makes for a wider, more realistic border.

15. Apply the cuff link to the edge of the French cuff. Use a small amount of water on back of the cuff link to help it stick.

16. Combine the luster dust with a few drops of vodka or clear extract until it's a paint-like consistency. Using a fine-tipped paintbrush, paint the cuff link with the bronze luster paint.

Pearls

PEARL-ENCRUSTED CAKES ARE QUICKLY BECOMING A MODERN WEDDING CLASSIC. In this version of the encrusted pearl design, a shortened center tier becomes the centerpiece, and I've used handmade fondant pearls and premade pearls for added dimension. While timeless for a wedding, this design would work beautifully for a milestone wedding anniversary celebration. Or, using the same encrusting technique, switch out the pearls for rainbow sprinkles to create a fun and modern birthday cake.

FOR THE CAKE

6 pounds ivory fondant

Approximately $1/2$ tsp. pearl luster dust

6-inch round and 10-inch round cakes, filled and crumb-coated (pp. 14–15; pp. 18–19)

8-inch round cake, with only one layer and crumb-coated

One 4-ounce container each 2-mm edible ivory pearls, 4-mm edible ivory pearls, and 6-mm edible ivory pearls

Cake-Making Tools (p. 10)

Small round cutters ($1/4$ inch, $1/2$ inch, 1 inch, $1^1/2$ inch)

Two parchment-paper-lined cookie sheets

Medium-sized plastic storage container with lid

Medium-sized mixing bowl

Piping gel

Paintbrush

TO MAKE THE PEARLS

NOTE: *The pearls may be made ahead of time and stored in an airtight container indefinitely.*

1. Roll out $1/4$ pound of ivory fondant to a $1/4$-inch thickness, then cut out approximately 40 to 50 circles using the $1/4$-inch round cutter. Pick up one of the circles and roll it between your hands to form a ball. Place the ball on a parchment-paper-lined cookie sheet. Repeat with the other $1/4$-inch circles.

2. Repeat Step 1 using $1/2$-inch, 1-inch, and $1^1/2$-inch cutters to create a nice variety of pearl sizes for the cake. Since you're starting with the same amount of fondant for each cutter, you'll end up with more of the smaller sizes and fewer of the larger sizes.

3. When the pearls have hardened on the outside but are still soft in the center (about 15 to 20 minutes), place them in a plastic container with the luster dust. Snap on the lid and gently shake the container to coat the pearls with luster dust. Store the pearls in the container for up to a month, or use immediately. Any leftover luster dust can be saved and reused.

TO DECORATE THE CAKE

1. Cover the cakes with the remaining ivory fondant following the method on p. 22, and dowel and stack them according to the directions on p. 26.

continued

2. In a medium-sized mixing bowl, combine a quarter of the 2-mm, 4-mm, 6-mm pearls, and the hand-rolled pearls. Mix them together with your hands to combine. I start with a small mix of pearls so that as I add them to the cake, I can add more or fewer of a size of pearl, depending on how the cake is coming along. It's nice to keep some of the reserved pearls separate so you can easily grab the size you need to fill in a space.

3. Place a turntable on a parchment-paper-lined cookie sheet and put the cake on the turntable. The cookie sheet will help catch any falling pearls as you apply them.

4. Apply the pearls in sections by the fistful. Start by brushing a 2- to 3-inch section of the 8-inch tier with a thin layer of piping gel. Scoop up a handful of the pearl mix and press it onto the piping gel. Work in sections to fill in the rest of the 8-inch cake, including the top.

5. Brush the piping gel $^1/_4$ inch up the 6-inch round cake and apply pearls by the handful. Cover the top edge of the 10-inch round with pearls in the same manner. Refill the pearl bowl when needed.

6. Fill in pearls wherever there are spaces on the 8-inch cake. This is an opportunity to arrange the pearls. Add in a few large ones where desired.

7. To finish the cake, add a few single pearls that trail up and down from the center tier. For these single pearls, brush the piping gel directly onto the pearl and use your fingers or tweezers to place them.

NOTE: *Because there so many pearls on the middle tier, I recommend removing the fondant from the tier before serving the slices. To do so, gently peel it away to reveal the crumb coat underneath. It should come off easily in one piece.*

SMALLER SHINDIGS

Create pretty pearl-encrusted cupcakes for smaller events or to serve alongside the larger cake.

- For a better texture, I suggest using pearls made of fondant when topping cupcakes as opposed to the crunchier edible pearls.
- For a pearl-covered look, roll a frosted cupcake in a bowl of pearls, or sprinkle the pearls on for a more airy look.

VARIATION

For a birthday celebration: You can create the same design but substitute rainbow sprinkles for the pearls.

CHAPTER 7

Special Occasions

HAVE CAKE, WILL PARTY! HOLIDAYS AND SPECIAL OCCASIONS ARE
a great excuse to create a festive cake. Many of the designs in this chapter
can easily be used for multiple occasions with just a few simple changes.
When baking for an occasion, get creative with your flavors and choose
cakes and fillings that reflect the season.

Make It Pretty Basics

Here are some tips that will help you with the cakes in this chapter.

- All of the cakes in this book are made up of four cake layers (baked in two pans and split in half), unless otherwise instructed.

- Use a brush of water to adhere fondant. Heavier pieces may require using piping gel, buttercream, or royal icing.

- In warmer months, working in an air-conditioned room is best. Finished cakes should be stored in the fridge overnight, or at room temperature if being served that day.

Monogram Trio

I'M SO LUCKY TO BE SURROUNDED BY CREATIVE PEOPLE WHO ARE IN THE WEDDING industry and who are so passionate about what they do. This cake trio was inspired by some amazing ladies I know who create letterpress invitations. Letterpress is an old style of relief printing that uses a printing press to print onto lush cotton-infused paper. I found inspiration for the font templates online. You don't have to use the same fonts I do; just find enough variety to create a similar collage feel.

FOR THE CAKE

$1/2$ pound gum paste

$1/2$ tsp. silver luster dust

Vodka or clear extract

Fine-tipped black food-color marker

Three 6-inch round cakes and one 8-inch round cake, filled and crumb-coated (pp. 14–15; pp. 18–19)

$6^1/2$ pounds white fondant

$1/2$ pound black fondant

Cake-Making Tools (p. 10)

$1/4$-inch round cutter

Parchment-paper-lined cookie sheet

Small bowl

Paintbrush

Printed monogram templates (font size between 64 and 96, depending on the font); (p. 154)

Piping gel

Grasscloth, burlap, or other tight, basketweave-style texture mat

TO MAKE THE TYPEWRITER KEYS

NOTE: *The letters and typewriter keys can be created ahead of time and stored in airtight containers.*

1. Roll out about an ounce of gum paste to $1/4$ inch thick, and cut out five circles using the $1/4$-inch cutter.

2. Use the fat end of a ball tool to indent all of the tops of the circles to create the shape of the typewriter key, and place the circles on a parchment-paper-lined cookie sheet to dry.

3. In a small bowl, mix the luster dust with a few drops of clear extract or vodka. Add just enough liquid to make the luster paint a spreadable consistency.

4. Use a small paintbrush to apply the luster paint to the circles. Set the cookie sheet aside to allow the silver to dry before handling the circles (15 to 20 minutes).

5. Roll out a grape-sized amount of gum paste so it's a little thinner than $1/8$ inch. Cut five circles from the gum paste using the $1/4$-inch round cutter. (The amount of gum paste needed will vary depending on the fonts and letters you're using.)

6. Apply the thin white circles to the middle of the dried silver circles to create the typewriter key. The silver edges should peek out from behind the white circle.

7. Use a black food-color marker to write an initial (or an ampersand) on the top of each typewriter key. Set the keys aside while you complete the cake design.

continued

TO CREATE MONOGRAMMED LETTERS

1. Make a template of the initials and ampersand you want to use on the cake in a font size that's large enough to use on the cake (about 64 to 96 points, depending on the font or the computer you're using). Print out the template. The letters on these cakes will be placed in squares that range in size from $3/4$ inch to $1^1/_2$ inches high, so when cutting out the letter template, don't follow the shape of the letter; instead, cut it out square. You are creating paper versions of the gum paste squares and rectangles that will go on your cake.

2. Roll out about 1 ounce of gum paste to $1/8$ inch thick. Place one of the letter templates on top and trim the gum paste to create a square the same size as the template.

3. With a knitting needle, trace the outline of the letter onto the gum paste square. Apply enough pressure to mark the gum paste, but not so much that you pierce the paper.

4. Lift off the paper template and trace over the indentations with a black food-color marker.

5. Repeat with other fonts and letters to create one of each of the letter initials and one each of the full monogram with ampersand. Set the completed gum paste squares on a parchment-paper-lined cookie sheet.

TO DECORATE THE CAKE

1. Cover the cakes with white fondant following the method on p. 22. Dowel and stack one of the 6-inch round cakes onto the 8-inch round cake according to the directions on p. 26.

2. Using a burlap or grasscloth texture mat, apply texture to the sides of all three cakes to create the effect of the white cotton paper that is used in letterpress and other fine stationery. To use the mat, place it against the side of one of the cakes and apply even pressure with one hand and use the other hand to keep it stable. Repeat on all sides of every cakes.

3. Apply the typewriter keys first; they are the focal point for each cake. Place one initial in the center front of both of the single 6-inch rounds. Apply the full monogram to the center of the top tier of the two-tier cake. Brush a small amount of water or piping gel onto the back of the key to adhere.

4. Brush a small amount of water onto the back of each square and press the single initials onto the 6-inch rounds. Apply the full monogram to the two-tier cake. There is no set pattern for applying the squares, so place them randomly, as if you were creating a collage.

5. To finish the cakes, use your hands (or an extruder) to roll the black fondant into three 19-inch ropes. Place the ropes around the bottom of each 6-inch cake.

MAKE IT *or* FAKE IT!

Use a food-color marker to write monograms or messages on strips of light-colored taffy. You can also use Smarties or similar wafer candy to make the typewriter keys.

VARIATIONS

For a more vibrant look:
Add color to the monograms by using one color for each of the initials. Use one color on one 6-inch cake and a different one on the other cake. Bring the two colors together on the monogram cake.

To create messages:
You can use the same font-tracing technique to create other kinds of celebration messages, like "Happy Birthday" or "Congratulations."

Presents & Pops

CREATING A CAKE FOR SOMEONE IS TRULY A MEANINGFUL GIFT, AND THE VARIATIONS ON present cake designs are endless—change the colors and these cakes can be created for any occasion, season, or celebration. I always suggest this style cake to people who want a special cake but aren't sure of their design direction.

The presents in this project would work beautifully on a winter party dessert buffet. Serve them alongside glittery white cake pops (similar to the pops I created while competing on the Food Networks' show *Sweet Genius*) to complete the wintery look. The pops are reminiscent of snowballs, while the sparkles and sugar pearls evoke the feeling of fresh fallen snow.

FOR THE CAKES

6-inch round cake and 6-inch square cake, filled and crumb-coated (pp. 14–15; pp. 18–19)

$3^1/2$ pounds light blue fondant

3 pounds of white fondant

Cake-Making Tools (p. 10)

Plastic wrap

$1/4$-inch and 2-inch round cutters

Parchment-paper-lined cookie sheet

Plastic piping bag filled with 1 cup of buttercream

Small paintbrush

Floral or scrolled texture mat

FOR THE CAKE POPS

1 dozen unfinished cake pops (see instructions on p. 17)

12-ounce bag white candy melts

Glass filled with premade edible pearls

Small microwave-safe bowl

White disco dust

Block of Styrofoam

Parchment-paper-lined cookie sheet

TO MAKE THE ROUND PRESENT

NOTE: *Ribbon loops should be made at least a day in advance so they can dry thoroughly.*

1. Cover the cake with $1^1/2$ pounds of light blue fondant according to the method on p. 22.

2. Roll out a quarter of the remaining blue fondant to $1/8$ inch thick, and cover it with plastic wrap. Then roll out $1/2$ pound of the white fondant to $1/8$ inch thick.

3. Remove the plastic from the blue fondant. Lay the blue fondant on top of the white fondant. Using a plastic rolling pin, gently roll the layered fondant to thin it down a little. Be careful not to roll so hard that the fondant thins too much or begins to marble.

4. Use a sharp knife or accordion cutter to cut seven strips that are 6 inches long by 1 inch wide, five strips that are 6 inches long by 1 inch wide, and three strips that are 2 inches long by 1 inch wide.

5. Use the ribbon loop technique for the bow tutorial on p. 40 to turn all the strips into loops. When making the loops, keep the white side out. Set them to dry on their sides with the loop open on a parchment-paper-lined cookie sheet.

continued

6. Cut two 3-inch-long by 1-inch-wide strips; pinch one end and trim the other end on a diagonal to look like the cut tails of a ribbon. Place them on the parchment-paper-lined sheet to dry.

7. Roll out $1/2$ pound of the remaining white fondant to $1/8$ inch thick, and cut circles from it using the $1/4$-inch and 2-inch round cutters. Randomly apply the circles to the cake.

8. When your bow loops are dry, begin the bow assembly by piping a small mound of buttercream (about half the size of a golf ball) on the center of the top of your cake.

9. Begin with the longest ribbon loops and stick the pointed end of each loop into the buttercream mound. Lay them flat against the cake so that the open part of the loop shows to the side. Place about seven loops in a circle to form the bottom layer of the bow.

10. Pipe another smaller mound (size of a grape) in the center of the first ribbon loop layer. Arrange the five shorter strips in the same manner as the first row.

11. Fill in the top of the bow with the three shortest strips, using buttercream to secure them where needed.

12. Slide the ribbon ends in between the bow rows wherever you feel they look best.

13. After the bow is assembled, use a small, dry paintbrush and gently pull away any visible buttercream that may be left around the bow loops.

TO MAKE THE SQUARE PRESENT

1. Cover the cake with the remaining 2 pounds of white fondant using the method on p. 22.

2. Roll the remaining blue fondant to $1/8$ inch thick. Gently press a texture mat onto the fondant surface to create a pattern.

3. Use a sharp knife or accordion cutter to cut four strips from the fondant that are 7 inches long by 2 inches wide each; these will be the ribbons for the sides of the cake.

4. Roll up the ribbon into a spool, and unroll it onto the cake from the bottom center of one side to the top center of the cake. Repeat with the other three ribbons on the other sides of the cake. Use a small brush of water to adhere where needed.

NOTE: *When working with textured fondant you want to press delicately so that you don't smudge the patterns created.*

5. Cut two more ribbons that are 4 inches long by 2 inches wide and $1/8$ inch thick. Pinch one end of each ribbon, and trim the other end into an upside down V, like a cut ribbon tail.

6. Place the pinched end on the center top of the cake. Lay one ribbon tail so that it rests between two of the ribbons that are wrapped around the cake. Allow it to bend and stand away from the cake at some points. Repeat on the other side using the other ribbon tail.

7. Use the bow technique described on p. 40 to create a textured fondant bow with loops that are about $2^1/2$ in. tall and 3 inches wide (after being folded) The ribbons should be 6 inches long and $2^1/2$ inches wide.

8. Set the bow on top of the cake so that the bow covers where the ribbon tails meet. The opening of the loop should face up, not out.

TO MAKE THE CAKE POPS

1. Melt white candy melts in a microwave-safe bowl. Microwave them in 30-second intervals, stirring after each, until smooth.

2. Dip a cake pop into the melted candy and gently tap the stick on the side of the bowl to shake off any excess.

3. While the candy melt covering is still wet, hold the pop over a parchment-paper-lined cookie sheet and sprinkle on white disco dust.

NOTE: *Dusting over the lined cookie sheet will enable you to reuse the excess disco dust.*

4. Place the pop into a piece of Styrofoam to set for about 10 to 15 minutes. Serve in a glass filled with edible pearls.

MAKE *it* BETTER

Use the scraps from the ribbon loop bow to create coiled streamers that can dress up the cake plates. Cut the scraps into $1/4$- to $1/2$-inch-wide strips (it doesn't matter how long they are or if they have rough edges). Wrap the strips around a wooden dowel and let them dry for 24 hours. Gently remove the coils from the dowel and place where needed.

Pup Cake

MY TWO-YEAR-OLD SON IS OBSESSED WITH ANIMALS. HE HAPPILY POINTS OUT EVERY dog, cat, or other furry creature to anyone who's nearby. Animal-themed birthday cakes are great for younger kids' parties or for a party that doesn't have a character theme. It's the perfect design for celebrations where both kids and adults are present. Bake the cake in a sophisticated flavor combo for the adults and make the cupcakes in various kid-pleasing flavors. Let them pick their favorite.

FOR THE CAKES

1 dozen cupcakes baked in brown wrappers

$1/2$ pound dark brown fondant

3 cups Vanilla Swiss Meringue Buttercream (recipe p. 198)

6-inch and 10-inch round cakes, filled and crumb-coated (pp. 14–15; pp. 18–19)

$1^1/2$ pounds white fondant

$2^1/2$ pounds bright blue fondant

1 pound each red, black, orange, green, and yellow fondant

$1^1/2$ pounds light brown fondant

4 ounces gray fondant (about the size of a grape)

Cake-Making Tools (p. 10)

Dog ear template (p. 162)

Parchment-paper-lined cookie sheet

Paintbrush

Docking tool

$1^1/2$-inch round cutter

Black food-color marker or letter cutter (for initial)

#2 piping tip

3-inch oval cutter

TO MAKE THE CUPCAKES

NOTE: *Make the dog ears at least a day ahead. They should dry completely so that they hold their shape when placed on the cupcakes.*

1. For rounded ears, trace two rounded ear templates (p. 162) onto a piece of paper and cut them out.

2. Roll out the dark brown fondant (or use light brown or white) to $1/8$ inch thick. Place the templates on the fondant and use a knitting needle to trace their shape. Cut out the ears with a sharp knife. Leave the ears plain, or add tiny dots of fondant in a contrasting shade. Make two ears for each cupcake.

3. Place the dog ears on a parchment-paper-lined cookie sheet to dry. Leave some ears flat and curl others over a thin wooden dowel to give the appearance of drooping ears when placed on the cupcake.

4. For triangular-shaped ears, roll out the fondant as previously described but use the triangular ear templates on p. 162 to cut out two ears. Trace the larger triangle in one color and the smaller triangle in a contrasting color. Use a little water to adhere the smaller triangle to the center of the larger one. Place the dog ears on a parchment-paper-lined cookie sheet to dry. Lay them flat to dry or curl the tips over a wooden dowel to bend them down.

5. On the day of the party, pipe the buttercream onto the cupcakes. Place the ears in the buttercream, and put the cupcakes in the refrigerator for at least 15 minutes so the ears can set in place. Set aside the cupcakes and finish the rest of your cake design.

continued

TO DECORATE THE TOP TIER

1. Following the directions on p. 22, cover the 6-inch cake using white fondant and the 10-inch cake using bright blue fondant. Dowel and stack them according to the directions on p. 26.

2. To decorate the top tier, roll out $1/2$ pound of the red fondant to $1/8$ inch thick. Use a sharp knife and ruler (or an accordion cutter) to cut a strip that's 19 inches long by $1^1/2$ inches wide to make the collar.

3. Roll up the strip into a scroll and apply it to the top tier of the cake about $1/2$ inch down from the top edge. Brush on a small amount of water to help it adhere, if necessary. Use the edge of a ruler to guide the strip straight. Run the docking tool along the top and bottom edges of the red strip to create the stitching lines.

4. Roll out 1 pound of the light brown fondant to $1/8$ inch thick, and use a small sharp knife to cut freehand spots ranging in size from 2 to 4 inches in diameter. Let the spots go wavy and try not to make them perfectly circular. Apply the brown spots randomly over the top tier.

5. To make the dog tag, roll out the gray fondant to $1/8$ inch thick. Cut a $1^1/2$-inch circle using the round cutter. Apply the circle to the front of the cake so that it overlaps a third of the red strip.

Rounded ear template

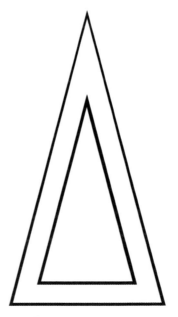

Triangular ear template

6. Use the tip of a #2 piping tip to cut a tiny circle into the top of the gray circle just inside the top edge. To create the ring that attaches the tag to the collar, roll a grape-sized amount of black fondant into a thin rope that's about the thickness of a piece of yarn. Trim a section from the rope that's about $1/2$ inch long. Insert one end of the rope into the small circle at the top of the gray circle. Attach the other end to the red strip.

7. Use a black food-color marker to write an initial, name, or message onto the dog tag. If using a letter cutter, roll a grape-sized amount of the black fondant to $1/8$ inch thick, and cut out the letter. Secure it to the dog tag using a small amount of water, if needed.

TO DECORATE THE BOTTOM TIER

8. To create the doghouses, choose a colored fondant (yellow, red, green, or orange) and roll it out to $1/8$ inch thick. Cut a rectangle that's between 3 and 4 inches long and $2^1/2$ to $3^1/2$ inches wide. At one end of the strip, trim the corners off at a diagonal to form the roof's peak. Apply the house to the cake with a little water, if needed.

9. Repeat Step 8 with each color, varying the heights and widths of the houses. Make approximately nine houses. Apply all of the houses before making the black fondant doghouse details. Use the back of your knife or a metal ruler to score lines about every $1/4$ inch onto the houses to give the illusion of siding.

10. To finish the houses, roll out the black fondant to $1/8$ inch thick. Cut out ovals, one for every dog house. Trim the bottom of the oval flat, and apply it to a house to create the door. Repeat for all of the houses.

11. To create the doghouse roofing, roll the remaining black fondant to $1/8$ inch thick. With a sharp knife and ruler (or an accordion cutter), cut thin black strips that are $1/8$ to $1/4$ inch wide. Apply the strips to the cake above each doghouse. First apply one side of the roof, and trim the strip straight up at the peak and flat at the end that hangs over the roof. Then do the same on the other side. Repeat for each doghouse.

12. To finish the cake, arrange the cupcakes on top of the cake. The remaining cupcakes can be placed on the table around the cake.

VARIATIONS

The variations on this cake theme are seemingly endless and equally adorable!

Jungle theme: Finish the cake tiers in an animal print or banana leaf patterns, then top the cupcakes with zebra, elephant, giraffe, and monkey ears.

Springtime celebration: Bake the cupcakes in pink and white wrappers and decorate the cake tiers with long grasses in varying shades of green. Decorate each cupcake with bunny-ear tops and place them on the cake.

Fiesta Cupcakes

WHILE BIG OVER-THE-TOP CAKES ARE GREAT, SOMETIMES THE SMALLER-SCALE DESIGNS are even more effective. For these cupcakes, I used simple images to immediately let guests know they have arrived at a fun fiesta!

FOR THE CUPCAKES

1 dozen cupcakes baked in green, red, or yellow wrappers and topped with buttercream

$1/2$ pound each yellow, orange, green, and red fondant

Vegetable shortening

4 ounces each white, black, pink, and brown fondant

Green and red food-color markers

$2^1/2$-inch round cutter

Three 9-ounce plastic cups (or any glass with a 2-inch diameter bottom)

Parchment-paper-lined cookie sheet

$1^1/2$-inch and $1/4$-inch five-petal blossom cutter

$1/2$-inch five-petal blossom cutter with pointed petals

Cake-Making Tools (p. 10)

TO MAKE THE SOMBREROS

1. Roll out half of the yellow fondant to slightly thicker than $1/8$ inch thick and use the $2^1/2$-inch cutter to cut three circles from the fondant.

2. Turn the plastic cups upside down and lightly rub the bottoms with vegetable shortening. Center and drape one circle over the bottom of each plastic cup, and use your fingers to fold the edges over the sides of the cup to create the rim of the sombrero. Allow them to set for 10 minutes before removing them from the cups. Place them rim side up on a parchment-paper-lined cookie sheet while you make the rest of the sombrero.

3. Roll a grape-sized piece of yellow fondant between your hands to create a ball. Taper one end of the ball into a rounded point to create the top of the sombrero, and then flatten the other end by gently pressing it against the table. Set the top of the sombrero into the center of one hat rim. Use a small amount of water to adhere it if necessary. Repeat to create two more hats.

4. Roll out about 2 ounces of white fondant to $1/4$ inch and cut from it strips that are 4 inches long and $1/4$ inch wide. Pick up one of the strips and wrap it around the base of the sombrero center. Trim away any excess fondant. Use the green and red food-color markers to draw stripes, zigzags, and dots onto the white stripes. Repeat for the other sombreros.

5. To make a mustache, pinch off two pea-sized pieces of black fondant. Roll one of the pieces between your fingers to create a teardrop shape. Turn the point of the teardrop up at the end. Repeat with the other piece of black fondant so that the turned up end is opposite the first piece.

continued

VARIATION

You can use the same idea to create cupcake toppers for any holiday.

Halloween: Use the sombrero technique to create witches hats out of black fondant.

New Year's Eve: Top hats are perfect for New Year's Eve cupcakes.

Kentucky Derby: Bonnets with flowers in pretty pastels would be a terrific addition to a Kentucky Derby party.

6. Set the sombrero on top of a frosted cupcake. Place the mustache just below the rim of the sombrero. The two rounded ends should face in, and the curled ends should face out.

TO MAKE THE FLOWERS

1. Roll out half of the orange fondant to $1/8$ inch thick. Cut out three flower shapes using the $1^1/2$-inch five-petal blossom cutter.

2. Place the cut flowers in the center of a plastic egg mold to curl the edges. Allow them to dry for at least an hour.

3. Use your fingers to roll three tiny pearls of green fondant, and place a pearl in the center of each flower. Secure them using a small amount of water, if needed. Place each flower on top of a frosted cupcake.

TO MAKE THE CACTUS

1. Roll 2 ounces of the green fondant into a log that is $1/2$ inch in diameter and 6 inches long.

2. Cut two 2-inch sections from the log to start the body of the cactus. Using your fingertips, round the top end of each cactus body to form the top.

3. Cut the remaining 2-inch section of fondant into two 1-inch logs and thin into ropes that are $1/4$ inch in diameter, and cut four 1-inch long sections from it. Using your fingertips, round each end of each of the 1-inch pieces.

4. Adhere two of the flat ends of each 1-inch piece onto either side of each cactus body to create the arms, and bend each arm up. Use a knitting needle to score short, wavy lines into each cactus to resemble the indentations in a real cactus.

5. Roll out a grape-sized amount of the pink fondant to $1/8$ inch thick. Use the $1/4$-inch five-petal blossom cutter to cut two flowers. Apply each flower to the cactus with a small amount of water. Press the flower onto the cactus using the tip of a knitting needle to create the indented center of the flower.

6. If you are using each cactus flat, as shown in the photo on p. 165, place it onto the cupcake right away. If you would like to stand the cacti up, allow them to dry for at least 3 hours before placing them into the frosted cupcakes.

TO MAKE THE CHILE PEPPER

1. Roll a grape-sized amount of red fondant between your hands to create a short, thick log. Apply more pressure to one end to taper the piece of fondant. The overall shape will be like a baby carrot, with one end thinner than the other.

2. Roll out about 2 ounces of green fondant to $1/4$ inch thick, and cut out a flower-shaped piece using the $1/2$-inch five-petal blossom cutter. Place the cut piece of green fondant over the fat end of the red chile pepper to create the leaves. Brush with a small amount of water to adhere it, if necessary.

3. To create a stem, pinch off a small piece of green fondant (about the size of a small pearl). Roll it into a tiny log to create the stem, and press it onto the end of the chile pepper. Repeat Steps 1 through 3 above to make the second chile pepper. Place each chile pepper on a frosted cupcake.

TO MAKE THE MARACAS

1. Roll a marble-sized piece of orange fondant between your hands to create an oval shape for the maraca. Repeat to make one more.

2. Pinch off a pea-sized piece of orange fondant from each oval you just rolled, and roll the smaller piece of fondant into a ball between your fingertips. Slightly squeeze each smaller ball to give it an oblong shape, and place it at the base of the maraca.

3. Roll a grape-sized piece of brown fondant into a thin rope about as thick as a piece of yarn. Cut four 1-inch pieces from the rope, and apply each to the base of a maraca to create the handle.

4. Roll out about 2 ounces of white fondant to $1/8$ inch thick. Use a sharp knife or accordion cutter to cut four $1/2$-inch-long by $1/4$-inch-wide by strips. Wrap one strip around the fat part of each maraca. Use a green food-color marker to draw a wavy line on each white strip. Place two maracas on each cupcake, and make sure the seam side is facing down.

Tattooed Heart

I LOVE TATTOO ART! BUT PERMANENT BODY ART IS EVERLASTING, SO TO ENJOY THE BEAUTY of this art form in a much less committed fashion, I created this classic tattoo-style "Mom" heart cake. The banner across the heart can be changed to a name or set of initials, which makes it a great Valentine's or anniversary cake. There are many free tattoo lettering templates on the Internet, so download your favorite one.

FOR THE CAKE

6-inch heart-shaped cake, filled and crumb-coated (pp. 14-15; pp. 18-19)

$1^{1}/_{2}$ pounds black fondant

$^{1}/_{4}$ pound red fondant

2 ounces gum paste

Black and red food-color markers

2 ounces green fondant

Cake-Making Tools (p. 10)

4-inch-wide heart cutter

1-inch leaf cutter

Lettering template printed to fit your banner (font size 64 to 72)

TO DECORATE THE CAKE

1. Cover the cake with black fondant according to the directions on p. 22.

2. To make the red heart, roll out the red fondant to $^{1}/_{4}$ inch thick, and cut it with the heart cutter. Place the heart on top of the cake in the center. Run your finger around the edges to soften the cut edge.

3. Roll out a strip of gum paste to $^{1}/_{8}$ inch thick. It should be large enough to cut an 8-inch by 2-inch rectangle. (This will become the banner.)

4. Brush a small amount of water across the heart where the banner will go. Place the banner diagonally across the center of the heart, and tuck each end under itself so that the ribbon's fold is visible. Fold the right side of the banner so that the curl is moving downward. Slightly curl the left side of the banner to face upward. Trim the ends of the banner with a sharp knife to create V-shaped banner tails.

5. Place your template on the banner and trace the outline of the letters with the tip of a knitting needle. Apply enough pressure to mark the surface of the gum paste, but do not pierce the paper.

6. Remove the paper template and outline the letters with a black food-color marker. Color in the letters with the red food-color marker.

continued

7. Outline the edges of the heart and the edges of the banner with the black food-color marker. This will give the design the tattoo feel.

8. Use the technique on p. 41 to make three ribbon roses. The ribbons for the cluster should be approximately 1 inch to 2 inches long. After they are completed, place the roses toward the top left side of the heart.

9. Roll out the green fondant to $1/4$ inch thick and cut two leaves. Pinch both ends of each leaf and place one on each side of the rose cluster. Outline the leaves with the black food color marker and draw in the center vein.

10. Use your fingers to roll any leftover black fondant into a $1/4$-inch-thick rope (about the thickness of licorice ropes). Trim two 2-inch-long and one 1-inch-long pieces from the rope. Taper one end of the rope and curl the other for each of the three pieces of rope. Place one of the longer curled ropes under the rose cluster with the tapered end under the rose cluster and the curl facing out. Place the shorter curled rope next to that one so that the curl faces the opposite direction. Add the last curl on the opposite side of the heart, just under the curve of the heart. Brush on a small amount of water to apply the curls if necessary.

Sweet & Sassy

THIS CAKE IS ALL GIRL AND ALL FUN, ALL THE TIME! BRIGHT COLORS, FLOWERS, RUFFLES, GLITTER, and animal print—I don't think I could include any more girly details on this cake design if I tried! Mini dress cakes look impressive but are deceptively simple to make. For a tamer affair, like a bridal shower or tea, make the front dress cake in white like the bride and the two cakes in the back in the colors of the bridesmaids' dresses. The fondant flowers can be created in the same colors that the bride and her bridal party will carry.

FOR THE CAKE

10-inch round cake, filled and crumb-coated (pp. 14–15; pp. 18–19)

2^1/$_2$ pounds hot pink fondant

2 pounds each black, purple, and yellow fondant

3 giant cupcakes, wrappers removed

2 cups buttercream

4 ounces each bright green and orange fondant

Cake-Making Tools (p. 10)

3-inch heart-shaped cutter

Two parchment-paper-lined cookie sheets

Paintbrush

Piping gel

Black disco dust

1-inch leaf cutter

Plastic wrap

Lollipop sticks

Four 2-mm edible white pearls (purchased or homemade; see p. 147)

2-inch five-petal flower cutter

1-inch five-petal flower cutter with pointed ends (or stephanotis cutter)

2-inch and ^{1}/$_2$-inch daisy cutters

^{1}/$_2$-inch round cutter

TO MAKE THE ZEBRA STRIPES

1. Cover the round cake with 2 pounds of the pink fondant using the method on p. 22.

2. Roll out 1 pound of the black fondant to ^{1}/$_8$ inch thick and cut wiggly strips that range from 2 to 4 inches long by ^{1}/$_4$ to 1 inch wide. Cut a few V-shaped squiggles, which are helpful when getting the zebra pattern started.

3. Apply a V-shaped squiggle to the middle of the side that will be the front of the cake. Brush on a small amount of water, if needed, to adhere.

4. Apply the other randomly shaped lines above and below the V. Take a look at the cake photo on p. 172 and note how the lines are placed—they don't touch, but they come close to one another. Animal patterns are supposed to be random, so don't stress about the zebra stripes.

TO MAKE THE MINI DRESSES

NOTE: *The heart-shaped bodices can be made up to 3 days in advance.*

1. At least 4 hours before decorating the cake, roll about 2 ounces of black, purple, and yellow fondant to ^{1}/$_4$ inch thick. Use the heart-shaped cutter to cut out one heart of each color. Place the hearts on the cookie sheet to dry.

2. Trim the top off one of the giant cupcakes so that it's flat. Keep the trimmed piece.

continued

3. Turn the cupcake over and spread a thin layer of buttercream over what was the bottom of the giant cupcake and is now the top. Place the rounded trimmed piece of cake on top. Trim away any cake that hangs over the edges. This is now the skirt portion of your mini dress cake.

4. Repeat with the other giant cupcakes. Crumb-coat and chill them for at least an hour.

To make the black dress
5. Roll out about 4 ounces of black fondant into a circle that's about 6 inches in diameter and cover the mini cake. Trim away the excess fondant at the bottom.

6. Use a sharp knife to make a small incision into the top of the mini cake where the bodice will go, and push the black fondant heart into the incision so that it stands upright.

7. To make the dress glittery, place it on a parchment-paper-lined cookie sheet, brush the cake with a thin coat of piping gel, and sprinkle black disco dust over the entire cake. Set it aside for 15 minutes to allow the piping gel to dry.

8. To make the flowers for the dresses, roll a small amount of green fondant, about an ounce, into a rectangle that is about 4 inches long by 2 inches wide by $1/8$ inch thick. Cut out 10 leaves; cover 7 in plastic wrap and set aside. Pinch one end of each of the three remaining green leaves. Using a brush of piping gel, apply two of the leaves to the lower right side of the black bodice so that the pinched ends are overlapping. Apply the other leaf to the top of the skirt opposite your first leaf cluster.

9. Make two orange and five pink ribbon roses following the technique on p. 41; use a pea-sized amount of fondant for each. Set three of the pink and one of the orange roses aside for the other dress cakes. Place the remaining two pink roses so they are one on top of the other in the center of the dress cake. Add the remaining orange one in between them to the right. Secure with a brush of piping gel. Place them so that they overlap the leaves.

10. Using the fondant flower technique on p. 37, make two yellow five-petal blossoms. Set one aside for the purple dress cake. Apply the remaining flower to the black dress with a brush of piping gel to the left of the pink ribbon roses. Add a pearl to the center, using piping gel again if needed.

continued

11. Using the technique from the bouquet cake on p. 110, make one purple mum. Tuck the mum behind the yellow fondant blossom. Set the dress aside.

To make the purple dress

12. Cover another mini dress cake with purple fondant and apply the heart-shaped bodice in the same manner as described previously. Roll out about 2 ounces of orange fondant to $1/4$ inch thick. Use the 2-inch five-petal blossom cutter to cut out seven orange flowers. Cut out the centers of the flowers using the $1/2$-inch round cutter. Apply one flower to the bodice of the cake and the others to the front and back of the dress skirt. Trim the flowers where they meet the edges of the bodice and skirt.

13. Pinch one end of one of the reserved green leaves. Brush a little piping gel onto the back of the leaf and place it toward the right side where the bodice meets the dress. Add the remaining yellow five-petal blossom to the base of the leaf to the right. Secure the flower to the dress and a pearl to the center of the flower with a brush of piping gel.

14. Apply two of the remaining pink ribbon roses and the orange ribbon rose in a cluster to the bottom edge of the dress toward the left side. Pinch the end of one of the remaining green leaves and tuck it behind the cluster with a brush of piping gel if needed. Set the dress aside.

To make the yellow dress

15. To decorate the remaining mini dress cake, roll out 1 pound of yellow fondant and follow the instructions for ruffle making on p. 42. Make ruffle strips that are about 5 inches long by 1 inch wide. Apply the ruffles to the bottom of the skirt, and allow the ruffles to overlap as you move up to the top of the cake. Insert the heart-shaped bodice into the top of the cake in the same manner as the other two dress cakes.

16. Pinch the ends of the last two green leaves and then pinch the ends together. Apply the leaves to the upper right hand side of the bodice so that the unpinched ends stick out over the edge. Add the last pink ribbon rose where the leaves are pinched together. Set the dress aside.

TO ASSEMBLE THE CAKE

17. Start with the black glittery dress cake. Place the dress mini cake onto a 10-inch round base by first spreading a dab of buttercream on the top of the cake toward what you want to be the front. Place the black glittery dress cake on the base cake so that the bottom edge of the dress is about an inch back from the edge. Place the purple dress cake behind the black one to the left and the yellow dress cake behind to the right. Secure the dress cakes to the base with a dab of buttercream.

18. Finish the bottom edge of the cake by rolling about 40 marble-sized black fondant pearls to place around the bottom edge; use the pearl technique on p. 147.

19. Use the remaining yellow, orange, pink, and purple fondant to create the cluster of flowers at the bottom of the base cake. Make one 2-inch-diameter hot pink ribbon rose (see p. 41), and two 1-inch-diameter orange ribbon roses to go on either side of it. Use the mum technique on p. 110 to create four purple mums. Place one on either side of the orange ribbon roses. Tuck in the remaining two to the right of the pink ribbon rose above and below the orange ribbon rose. Follow the fondant flower technique from p. 37 to make two small yellow five-petal blossoms. Place the yellow flowers on the top and to the left of the pink ribbon rose. Place a white pearl in the center of each flower. When placing flowers and the pearl centers, secure with a brush of piping gel, if needed.

Stars & Stripes

INSPIRED BY THE BOWS AND BUNTING THAT DECORATED PARADE ROUTES IN YEARS PAST, this cake's muted tones of burgundy and navy add an elegant feel to what is typically a casual holiday. The bunting technique in this design is extremely versatile. You can swap in school colors to create bunting for a fun graduation cake or use primary colors to create a cake with a circus feel.

FOR THE CAKE

6-inch, 8-inch, and 10-inch round cakes, filled and crumb-coated (pp. 14–15; pp. 18–19)

8 pounds ivory fondant

2 pounds each burgundy and navy fondant

Piping bag filled with 1 cup of buttercream

$1/4$ tsp. bronze luster dust

Vodka or any clear extract

Cake-Making Tools (p. 10)

Plastic wrap

$1/4$-inch star cutter

Two parchment-paper-lined cookie sheets

Paintbrush

1-inch silicone button mold (or a 1-inch round cutter)

Small bowl

Set of Ateco round cutters

TO MAKE THE BOW

1. Use 6 pounds of the ivory fondant to cover the cakes using the method on p. 22, and dowel and stack the cakes according to the directions on p. 26.

2. Roll out $1/2$ pound of the remaining ivory fondant to $1/8$ inch thick and cover it with plastic wrap. Roll out 1 pound of the navy fondant to $1/8$ inch thick. Remove the plastic wrap from the ivory fondant and lay the navy fondant on top of the ivory fondant. Gently smooth the navy fondant with your hands so that the two stick together, making sure there aren't any air bubbles.

3. Use the star cutter to cut a star pattern into the navy fondant. Use enough pressure to cut through the navy fondant, but not so much that you cut through the ivory fondant. Use a scalpel or X-ACTO knife to gently lift out the cut navy stars.

4. From the layered ivory and navy fondant, cut strips in the following measurements:
- Three strips that are 2 inches wide by 5 inches long
- Two strips that are 2 inches wide by 4 inches long

NOTE: *Work quickly and carefully with the layered fondant so that you don't warp or crack the star pattern.*

5. Turn the strips into ribbon loops using the directions on p. 40. Place the loops on a parchment-paper-lined cookie sheet while you work on the rest of the cake. Leave them flat to dry, not open on their sides like a package bow. You will apply the loops while they are still soft and pliable, so make them on the same day you will decorate your cake. *continued*

6. Roll out $^1/_2$ pound of the remaining ivory fondant to $^1/_8$ inch thick. Roll out 1 pound of the burgundy fondant to $^1/_8$ inch thick. Use a sharp knife and ruler (or an accordion cutter) to cut $^1/_4$-inch-wide strips from the burgundy fondant. Lay the strips on the ivory fondant, spacing them an even $^1/_4$ inch apart to create a striped pattern. Use a rolling pin to gently press the burgundy strips to the ivory fondant.

7. From the layered striped fondant, cut strips in the following measurements:
- Two tail strips that are 3 inches wide by 5 inches long
- Two strips that are 3 inches wide by 4 inches long
- Four strips that are 2 inches wide by 3 inches long

8. Set the strips for the tail aside, and cover them with plastic wrap to keep them from drying out. Turn the remaining strips into ribbon loops according to the directions on p. 40. Let the loops dry on a parchment-paper-lined cookie sheet as you did for the star loops in Step 5.

9. Uncover the two tail strips and pinch them at one end as you do when starting a bow. Cut an upside-down V from the other end to create the ribbon tail.

10. Position the tails so that the pinched ends are about halfway up from the bottom of the top cake tier and touching each other. Drape the ends so that they hang over the top edge of the middle tier. Brush a small amount of water on the back of the tails to help them adhere.

11. Squeeze a dime-sized dab of buttercream onto the back of one of the longest star loops to attach it to the side of the cake. The loop should stick up over the top edge of the cake, and the point should just touch the top of one of the tails. To help secure the bow loop, hold it gently against the cake with one hand, and with your other hand, slide a small metal spatula inside the bow loop, using it to press the back of the bow loop to the cake. This helps prevent damaging the texture pattern on the front of the bow loop.

12. Apply two more navy star loops, one on each side of the first loop, using the technique described in Step 11. Apply the largest striped loop opposite the first loop you placed on the cake, without covering the tails (see Bow Figure 1).

13. Add a quarter-sized amount of buttercream over the tips of the ribbon loops from the first row. While this will help secure the next row, you will still need to add a small amount of buttercream to the back of each loop before applying it. Add two of the smaller striped loops on top of the larger navy loops and a star loop on top of the larger burgundy loop. Tuck the remaining burgundy loops between the larger blue loops toward the top of the cake. Tuck the last navy star loop behind the larger burgundy loop (see Bow Figure 2). Feel free to layer the loops as you like. It doesn't have to be exactly as I created it; just make sure to alternate the color and pattern for a textured feel.

14. Roll out a golf-ball-sized amount of ivory fondant to $1/4$ inch thick. Cut the fondant into $1/2$-inch-wide strips and create a ruffle according to the directions on p. 42 to finish the center of the loop. There should be buttercream still exposed from applying the ribbon loops for the ruffle to adhere to. Use the fat end of a ball tool to press the ruffle into the center of the bow (see Bow Figure 3).

15. Using a grape-sized amount of ivory fondant (about 2 ounces), make a button for the center of your bow. You can make the button by using a silicone button mold and following the instructions on p. 44, or you can cut a 1-inch circle from a piece of ivory fondant that was rolled out to $1/4$ inch thick. Mix the luster dust with a few drops of vodka or extract to create paint and paint the button with it. Pipe a tiny pearl of buttercream into the center of the ruffle, and push the button into the middle of the bow.

continued

Bow Figure 1

Bow Figure 2

Bow Figure 3

Bunting Figure 1

Bunting Figure 2

Bunting Figure 3

Bunting Figure 4

TO MAKE THE BUNTING

NOTE: *The bunting is made by creating one finished piece at a time. If you were to roll all of the circles at once, the fondant would dry out too quickly and crack or ripple when you try to work with it.*

1. Roll out about 4 ounces of the ivory fondant to $1/8$ inch thick. Cut from it a 5-inch circle and cover it with plastic wrap. Do the same with a piece of burgundy fondant. Remove the plastic wrap from the ivory circle, and lay the burgundy circle on top of the ivory one. Use a $3^1/_2$-inch round cutter to cut through the center of the burgundy fondant; don't cut through the ivory layer. Remove the burgundy circle from the middle to expose the ivory fondant. Cover the burgundy and ivory circle with plastic wrap.

2. Roll about an ounce of navy fondant to $1/8$-inch thick and cut out a $1^1/_2$-inch circle. Remove the plastic wrap from the ivory and burgundy circle and place the navy circle in the center of it. Very gently roll a plastic rolling pin over the circle to make sure the pieces stick together—just don't warp the circle or pattern. If the circle loses its shape at all, use the 5-inch circle cutter to recut the edges back into a perfect circle.

NOTE: *Creating the striping on the circle is easier using this method, because it is very difficult to move a circle once the middle has been cut from it. It would lose its shape and not give the clean crisp feel you're going for.*

3. Use a sharp knife to cut a V-shaped wedge from the circle— just as you would cut a slice of pizza (see Bunting Figure 1). The wedge should be about a fifth of the size of the circle. Discard the wedge or save it to use as a cupcake topper.

4. Place the circle in front of you so that the area where the wedge was cut is at the top. Slide a knitting needle under the circle from the bottom toward the center. To create the center ripple in the bunting, use the knitting needle to pull the fondant up slightly, allowing the sides of the circle to drape down (see Bunting Figure 2).

5. Repeat the rippled technique to the right of the center ripple (see Bunting Figure 3). The top edge of where the wedge was cut should now be close to horizontal. Repeat on the opposite side (see Bunting Figure 4).

6. Use a sharp knife to trim the top edge of the bunting to create a crisp horizontal line.

7. Apply the bunting to the cake along the top edge of the bottom tier. Brush the area of the cake with a little water or piping gel. With one hand, gently position the bunting into place; with your other hand, press the flat portions of the bunting against the cake to firmly adhere. Repeat this process all around the cake.

NOTE: *Even though the bunting is a little on the heavy side, I prefer to use water or piping gel rather than buttercream so that the bunting lies directly against the surface of the cake.*

TO MAKE THE TWISTED ROPE

1. Using your hands or an extruder, roll each color of the remaining fondant into a $1/4$-inch-thick rope that's about 32 inches long.

2. Lay the ropes next to each other and pinch them all together at both ends. Twist the ropes together starting at the ends, working your way toward the center.

3. Wrap the rope around the base of the bottom tier and brush on a small amount of water to adhere it, if needed.

SMALLER SHINDIGS

If an Independence Day wedding isn't part of your plans, you can still make an elegant dessert to celebrate the day.

- You can create pretty bunting cupcake toppers. Bake the cupcakes in wrappers that are red, white, and blue. Make the bunting circles but don't cut the wedges from the middle—leave the circle whole. Use a knitting needle to lift the fondant in places around the circle to create ripples around the edges.
- You can also make cupcake toppers using the layered fondant techniques from the bow. Layer the fondant in the same way, but instead of creating ribbon loops, cut circles from the layered fondant and use them to top frosted cupcakes. Then, arrange the cupcakes on a platter to create a flag shape.

Tailgate Cake

THIS IS A GREAT CAKE TO SERVE FOR A BIG GAME, BUT IT'S ALSO A GREAT DESSERT AT A SUMMER barbeque. The cake gives you plenty of servings for a big crowd, while the cupcakes provide a convenient self-serve option.

FOR THE PENNANT

$1/2$ pound orange fondant

2 ounces white fondant

2 sheets of parchment paper

Masking tape

Docking tool

Black food-color marker

FOR THE GRILL CAKE

Two 8-inch round cakes, filled and crumb-coated (pp. 14–15; pp. 18–19)

$2^1/2$ pounds gray fondant

4 pounds white fondant

Black gel food color

$1/2$ cup black sprinkles

$1/2$ pound each black and brown fondant

2 ounces pink fondant

2 pounds red fondant

$1/2$ pound vanilla buttercream

6-inch round cake pan

Cake-Making Tools (p. 10)

$1/4$-inch, 1-inch, 2-inch, and 3-inch round cutters

Parchment-paper-line cookie sheet

1 sheet of parchment paper

Extruder (optional)

Paintbrush

Foam craft brush

Five wooden dowels (for grill grates)

Burlap texture mat

Piping gel

14-inch square cake drum

continued

TO MAKE THE PENNANT

NOTE: *The pennant can be made a day or two in advance so it has time to dry thoroughly and hold its wavy shape.*

1. Roll up two sheets of parchment paper and secure them with masking tape to create two paper tubes. Set them aside. You will dry the fondant pennant over these to give it waves.

2. Roll out the orange fondant to $1/8$ inch thick, large enough to cut out a 6-inch by $3^1/2$-inch rectangle.

3. Mark the center of the rectangle at one end, and from that mark, cut a diagonal line toward each opposite corner to create the pennant shape.

4. Roll out the white fondant to $1/8$ inch thick, large enough to cut a strip that's $3^1/2$ inches long by $1/4$ inch wide. Line up the white strip of fondant with the wide edge of the orange pennant to create the binding and trim any areas that hang over the edge.

5. Roll the docking tool about $1/4$ inch inside the pennant edge and along both sides of the white strip to give it a "stitched" look.

6. Write a message on the pennant with a food-color marker, then lay the pennant across the paper tubes to dry. (The waves of the pennant make it difficult to write on after it dries.) Set the pennant aside.

TO MAKE THE GRILL CAKE

1. To make the indentation for the grill, place the 6-inch round cake pan on top of one of the 8-inch cakes.

2. Use a small sharp knife to trace the outline of the cake pan onto the cake. Remove the pan and cut through the first layer of the cake, following the outline of the 6-inch round circle. Remove the circle of cake and discard.

continued

FOR THE CUPCAKES

6 cupcakes frosted with vanilla buttercream (four baked in black wrappers, one in a red wrapper, and one in a yellow wrapper)

2 ounces each pale green, bright green, and white fondant

$1/2$ pound each red and yellow fondant

2 mini cupcakes

Two parchment-paper-lined cookie sheets

Cake-Making Tools (p. 10)

3. Cover the trimmed cake with 2 pounds of gray fondant according to the directions on p. 22, then smooth out the fondant, starting with the top and sides of the indented part of the cake, followed by the sides of the cake.

4. Cover the untrimmed cake with 2 pounds of white fondant according to the directions on p. 22. Dowel and stack the gray cake on top of the white cake according to the directions on p. 26. Having the same-sized tiers does not affect the stacking.

5. Add the legs to the grill by rolling out $1/2$ pound of the gray fondant to $1/4$ inch thick. Cut two 4-inch by 2-inch strips.

6. Place the strips for the legs by adhering the top of the strip just above where the gray and white cakes meet. The legs should be placed about 3 inches apart from one another and tilt slightly from the center out. Where the strips connect to the "grill," gently mark the center of the strip with the $1/4$-inch round cutter, and use a ball tool to make a small indentation in the center of the circle.

To make the spatula

7. Make the spatula base with the gray fondant you have already rolled out. Cut a 3-inch by $1^1/2$-inch rectangle. Measure $2^1/2$ inches down from the top of the rectangle and mark each edge at that point. Next, measure $1/2$ inch in across the top from each top edge and mark that point. Cut a diagonal line from each point to cut off the top two corners of the rectangle. There should still be a $1/2$-inch-wide area at the top of the rectangle between the two areas you just cut.

8. Use the back of a knife to gently score a line parallel to the top of the spatula and bend the fondant up slightly along that line to create the bend in the spatula. Place it on the lined cookie sheet so that the bent portion is resting against the wall of the cookie sheet. Make three indentations in the flat side of the fondant spatula using your small metal spatula with the tapered end. Set the fondant spatula base aside and allow it to dry for at least an hour.

NOTE: *The base of the spatula can be made ahead of time and stored until you make the cake.*

9. Make the handle of the spatula by cutting a 1-inch round circle from the rolled-out gray fondant. Using the $1/4$-inch round cutter, cut out the center of that circle. Apply the 1-inch

circle to the top left side of the gray cake. Cut a 3-inch by
$1/4$-inch strip from the same gray fondant and attach it to the
cake so that it comes straight down from the circle.

10. Gather the remaining gray fondant and using your hands
or an extruder, roll a rope that's $1/4$ inch in diameter and a little
longer than 20 inches.

11. Pinch off 1 inch of the rope. Brush a small amount of water
in the center of the hole at the end of the spatula handle.
Place one end of the small rope in the hole, attaching it to the
cake. Bend the rest of it up to create the hook that the spatula
hangs on.

To finish the grill

12. Brush a thin line of water around the top edge of the
indented part of the grill and apply the gray rope to it.

13. Use a foam craft brush and black gel food color to paint the
wooden dowels that will be used for the grill grate, then set
them on parchment paper to dry.

14. Before adding the grill grate, pour the black sprinkles into
the cut-out portion of the cake. This is the "charcoal."

15. To form the grill grate, press one end of the dowel inside
the inner wall of the cut-out part of the cake. Push the other
end of the dowel into the opposite wall and slide the dowel
slightly so that it's even on both sides. Continue with two more
dowels on either side.

16. Add the wheels to the grill by rolling out the black fondant
to about $1/4$ inch thick. Cut out two circles with the 3-inch
round cutter. Apply the circles to the base of the grill legs. Use
the 1-inch and $1/4$-inch round cutters to make marks in the
center of each wheel. Use a ball tool to make an indentation in
the center of each wheel.

To make the hamburgers and hot dogs

17. Make the hamburgers by dividing the brown fondant in
half. Roll each half into a ball and form a "patty" between your
hands. Give the burgers a meaty look by marking up the top
and sides using the burlap texture mat. Place the burgers on
the grill.

continued

18. Make the hot dogs by dividing the pink fondant in half. Roll each piece in your hands to create a log, and round each end with your fingers. Bend the log slightly in the center to look like a hot dog. Place the dogs on the grill as well.

19. Use a small paintbrush and black gel food color to brush "grill marks" on the burgers and hot dogs.

To make the checkerboard cake board

20. To make the checkerboard cake board, roll out the red fondant and the remaining white fondant to $1/8$ inch thick. Use a sharp knife and ruler or an accordion cutter to cut both pieces of fondant into 2-inch squares. Brush the surface of the board sparingly with piping gel so that the checkerboard pieces will stick.

21. Start in one corner of the square cake drum and place a white square so that it's flush with both sides. Place the red square next to it. Continue alternating red and white squares until you reach the end of the board. Trim the last piece at the other edge of the board.

22. Start the next row but place the red square first; alternate the square colors across the rest of the board until it is covered.

23. Use a small metal spatula to smear a golf-ball-sized amount of buttercream onto the board and place the grill cake on top.

24. Once the cake is placed on the board, you can finish the spatula by applying the base to the end of the handle. Brush the cake with a small amount of water to adhere if necessary.

TO MAKE THE CONDIMENT CUPCAKES

1. To make the relish, roll out both shades of green fondant to about $1/4$ inch thick.

2. Use a sharp knife to slice both pieces of fondant into thin, uneven strips. Then slice them again in the opposite direction, creating little cubes of pale and bright green fondant.

3. Scoop up the little cubes of green fondant and place them on a parchment-paper-lined cookie sheet until needed.

4. To make the tomatoes, use 2 ounces of red fondant and repeat Steps 1 through 3 for the relish.

5. To make the onion pieces, roll out the white fondant to $1/4$ inch thick and score lines across it with the back of your knife before cutting into cubes as you did for the relish and the tomatoes.

6. To make the shredded cheese, roll out 2 ounces of yellow fondant to $1/8$ inch thick. With a sharp knife, cut very thin strips, about $1/8$ inch wide, to the same thickness as shredded cheese. Cut the strips into pieces that are approximately 1 inch long. Gather the pieces with your fingers and then let them fall back again to the table to create the look of shredded cheese.

7. Cover the frosted cupcakes that were baked in a black wrapper with toppings. Fill the palm of one hand with all the relish pieces, then pick up the cupcake and turn it frosting side down into your hand filled with relish pieces. Gently roll the cupcake around so that it gathers up as many pieces as possible. Turn the cupcake back over and add any more pieces of relish as needed. Repeat the same process with the other condiments.

8. To make the ketchup container, roll out the remaining red fondant to $1/8$ inch thick. Place the piece of rolled fondant over one of the mini cupcakes and press the fondant so that it sticks to the top and sides of the mini cupcake. Trim away any excess. Set the mini cupcake aside.

9. Roll out a small piece of red fondant to $1/4$ inch thick. Cut a 1-inch circle, and place it on top of the covered mini cupcake.

10. Roll a grape-sized piece of leftover red fondant into a log about 1 inch long. Apply more pressure to one end so that it is slightly tapered. Trim the wider end of the log so that it is flat. Brush a small amount of water onto the top of the covered mini cupcake and place the log standing up in the center, tapered end up. Using a knitting needle, make a hole at the end of the log, creating the ketchup squirt nozzle.

11. Set the completed mini cupcake on top of the frosted cupcake baked in the red wrapper.

12. To make the mustard container, repeat Steps 8 through 11 but with yellow fondant and the cupcake baked in the yellow wrapper. Place all the finished condiment cupcakes on the cake board.

PART THREE

Recipes

8

Bake It!

GREAT CAKES START FROM THE INSIDE OUT! THE TASTE OF THE
cake should impress just as much as its design. I've developed my recipes over many years, most of them during my time as a restaurant pastry chef. The cakes taste great and their texture is perfect for stacking and decorating—you simply won't get the same taste or form from a box mix.

The key to avoiding a baking disaster is reading the instructions all the way through first. This will save you from doing something you really shouldn't. Gather your tools and ingredients ahead of time to make the process more efficient. Pay close attention to time and temperature recommendations, because they really do affect the baking process. And always use the proper tools for the job (see the "Better Baking Tools" section and sidebars in Chapter 1). If you aren't in the mood to bake, you can always fake it—stop by a bakery and buy a premade, undecorated cake to use as your base.

Vanilla Chiffon Cake

LIGHT, FLUFFY, AND MOIST, CHIFFON CAKE IS CLASSICALLY MADE WITH SEPARATED EGGS and uses oil as the fat. The secret to this cake is to divide the eggs, whip the whites, and fold them into the batter to lighten it. A true chiffon cake is made with only oil, but the flavor of butter just can't be beat, so here I combine the two. The color of the cake is not quite "white" and not quite "yellow," but trust that it is 100% delicious!

One of the many reasons I love this recipe is that it can be made without a mixer (that is, if you don't mind using a bit of elbow grease to get those egg whites whipped). I also love it because the flavor is so easy to vary by adding just a few ingredients. Some of my favorite variations include blueberry lemon, ginger, and orange clove.

MAKES TWO 8-INCH ROUND CAKES

Cooking spray

$2^{1}/_{2}$ cups cake flour; more for the pans

$1^{1}/_{2}$ cups granulated sugar

$1^{1}/_{4}$ tsp. baking powder

$^{1}/_{4}$ tsp. baking soda

1 tsp. kosher salt

6 large egg yolks

4 ounces (1 stick) unsalted butter, melted and cooled slightly

2 Tbs. vegetable oil

2 tsp. pure vanilla extract

1 cup buttermilk

3 large egg whites

1. Position a rack in the center of the oven and heat the oven to 350°F. Spray two 8-inch round pans with cooking spray and flour them.

2. In a large bowl, combine the cake flour, sugar, baking powder, baking soda, and salt. Whisk to combine.

3. In a medium bowl, whisk together the egg yolks, melted butter, vegetable oil, and vanilla extract. Once combined, whisk in the buttermilk. (The buttermilk goes in last so that it doesn't cause the melted butter to coagulate and create lumps.)

4. In the bowl of a stand mixer fitted with the whisk attachment (or in a large bowl using an electric hand mixer or a hand-held whisk), whisk the egg whites on medium-high speed until stiff peaks form, 5 to 7 minutes.

5. Pour the bowl of wet ingredients into the bowl of dry ingredients and fold them together with a rubber spatula until combined.

6. Using the spatula, gently fold the egg whites into the cake batter in three batches. Take care not to deflate the egg whites or overmix the batter.

7. Divide the batter evenly between the prepared pans. Bake until a toothpick inserted in the center of a cake comes out clean or with a few moist crumbs clinging to it, 25 to 30 minutes.

8. Transfer the cakes to a rack to cool in the pan for about 30 minutes. To invert, run a knife or thin metal spatula around the edge of one cake to help loosen it. Invert the cake onto a plate. Remove the cake pan. Place a cake plate on top of the cake, and invert it again so the cake plate is on the bottom. Repeat for the other cake. Let the cakes cool completely before filling, frosting, or storing. Once cool, the unfrosted cakes can be wrapped in plastic wrap and refrigerated for up to 2 days.

Vanilla Chiffon Cake with Vanilla Swiss Meringue Buttercream

VARIATIONS

BLUEBERRY-LEMON CHIFFON CAKE
Before folding in the egg whites, stir in $1\frac{1}{2}$ Tbs. fresh lemon zest (from about 1 large lemon) and $\frac{1}{2}$ cup of fresh or frozen blueberries. (I use frozen wild Maine blueberries or fresh when available.)

GINGER CHIFFON CAKE
Before folding in the egg whites, stir in 1 Tbs. ground ginger and $\frac{1}{4}$ cup ginger preserves. (Ginger preserves are available in the jam aisle of most grocery stores.)

ORANGE-CLOVE CHIFFON CAKE
Before folding in the egg whites, stir in 2 Tbs. orange zest (from about 1 orange) and $\frac{1}{2}$ tsp. ground cloves.

Devil's Food Cake

DEVIL'S FOOD CAKE WAS ONE OF THE FIRST CAKE RECIPES I LEARNED AS A PASTRY CHEF.
It's a great go-to recipe for birthday cakes and cupcakes, and the flavor appeals to
adults and kids alike. Pair it with vanilla buttercream for a classic chocolate/vanilla
combination, or layer in a salted caramel filling or blackberry cabernet buttercream for
a more sophisticated flavor profile. For this recipe, the key ingredient is obviously the
cocoa powder, so, as always, use the best quality you can find. Dutch-processed cocoa
will yield the best results. I also prefer dark brown sugar, which provides a more complex
sweetness than light brown sugar.

MAKES TWO 8-INCH ROUND CAKES OR 2 DOZEN CUPCAKES

Cooking spray

4 cups unbleached all-purpose flour;
more for the pans

8 ounces (2 sticks) unsalted butter,
softened

2½ cups dark brown sugar

1½ cups granulated sugar

8 large eggs

1½ cups unsweetened cocoa powder,
preferably Dutch processed

1 cup whole milk

2 tsp. baking soda

2 tsp. kosher salt

1. Position a rack in the center of the oven and heat the oven
to 350°F. Spray two 8-inch round pans with cooking spray and
flour them. (If making cupcakes, line 24 standard-sized muffin
cups with paper liners.)

2. In the bowl of a stand mixer fitted with the paddle
attachment (or in a large bowl using an electric hand mixer),
beat the butter, dark brown sugar, and granulated sugar
together at medium speed until fluffy and lighter in color,
stopping to scrape down the sides of the bowl with a rubber
spatula to make sure there are no butter lumps, about
5 minutes.

3. Add the eggs one at a time until completely combined.

4. Put the cocoa powder in a medium heatproof bowl. Pour in
2 cups of hot tap water and whisk to dissolve the cocoa powder.
Whisk in the milk and set aside.

5. In a separate medium bowl, combine the flour, baking soda,
and salt.

6. Slowly add about one-third of the dry ingredients to the
butter mixture and mix on low speed until incorporated.
Continue adding the dry and wet ingredients one-third at a
time, alternating between the two and ending with the dry
ingredients, stopping occasionally to scrape down the sides of
the bowl with a rubber spatula.

7. Divide the cake batter evenly between the prepared cake pans (or muffin tins) and bake, rotating the pans' positions halfway through baking, until a toothpick inserted in the center of a cake comes out clean or with a few moist crumbs clinging to it, 25 to 30 minutes (15 to 18 minutes for cupcakes).

8. Transfer the cakes to a rack to cool in the pan for about 30 minutes. To invert, run a knife or thin metal spatula around the edge of one cake to help loosen it. Invert the cake onto a plate. Remove the cake pan. Place a cake plate on top of the cake, and invert it again so the cake plate is on the bottom. Repeat for the other cake. Transfer cupcakes to a rack to cool in the pans for about 10 minutes before turning them out onto a plate or countertop.

9. Let the cakes cool completely before frosting or storing. Once cool, the unfrosted cakes can be wrapped in plastic wrap and refrigerated for up to 2 days. (Cupcakes are best when frosted and served the day they're baked.)

Devil's Food Cake with Chocolate Ganache and Peanut Butter Frosting

Pumpkin Spice Cake

FALL IS A TERRIFIC TIME FOR BAKING, SINCE THERE ARE SO MANY INSPIRING SEASONAL flavors to choose from. I introduced this cake to my clients a few years ago as an alternative to traditional carrot cake. It has a nice structure but stays super moist, making it a great choice for decorating. Pair it with cream cheese frosting for a sweet-tangy flavor combo.

MAKES TWO 8-INCH ROUND CAKES

Cooking spray

3 cups cake flour; more for the pans

2 tsp. baking powder

1 tsp. baking soda

1½ tsp. ground cinnamon

1 tsp. ground ginger

½ tsp. kosher salt

¼ tsp. ground allspice

⅛ tsp. ground cloves

4 large eggs

2 cups granulated sugar

One 15-ounce can pure pumpkin purée

1 cup vegetable oil

1 tsp. pure vanilla extract

1. Position a rack in the center of the oven and heat the oven to 350°F. Spray two 8-inch round pans with cooking spray and flour them.

2. In a large bowl, combine the cake flour, baking powder, baking soda, cinnamon, ginger, salt, allspice, and cloves. Whisk to combine.

3. In a separate medium bowl, whisk together the eggs, sugar, pumpkin purée, vegetable oil, and vanilla extract.

4. Pour the wet mixture into the dry ingredients and whisk until combined. If the batter becomes too thick to whisk, switch to a rubber spatula. Stir until the flour is completely incorporated.

5. Divide the batter evenly between the prepared pans.

6. Bake until a toothpick inserted in the center of a cake comes out clean or with a few moist crumbs clinging to it, 30 to 35 minutes.

7. Transfer the cakes to a rack to cool in the pan for about 30 minutes. To invert, run a knife or thin metal spatula around the edge of one cake to help loosen it. Invert the cake onto a plate. Remove the cake pan. Place a cake plate on top of the cake, and invert it again so the cake plate is on the bottom. Repeat for the other cake. Let the cakes cool completely before filling, frosting, or storing.

8. Once cool, the unfrosted cakes can be wrapped in plastic wrap and refrigerated for up to 2 days.

Pumpkin Spice Cake with Cream Cheese Frosting

Hazelnut Cake

SURPRISE YOUR GUESTS (AND YOURSELF) WITH THIS DELICIOUSLY DIFFERENT CAKE; IT'S lovely as a layered cake on its own or with just a dusting of powdered sugar. Hazelnut paste is a specialty ingredient that's available in high-end supermarkets and online (note that hazelnuts are sometimes called filberts, so be on the lookout for filbert paste as well). If you can't find it, this recipe also works well with any nut butter or paste. If you use peanut butter, however, be sure to use a low- or no-sugar-added natural version.

MAKES TWO 8-INCH ROUND CAKES

Cooking spray

1 cup cake flour; more for the pans

8 ounces (2 sticks) unsalted butter, softened

1 cup granulated sugar

1 cup hazelnut paste

6 large eggs

1 tsp. pure vanilla extract

1/2 tsp. kosher salt

1 tsp. baking powder

Hazelnut Cake with Toffee Buttercream and Salted Caramel

1. Position a rack in the center of the oven and heat the oven to 350°F. Spray two 8-inch round pans with cooking spray and flour them.

2. In the bowl of a stand mixer fitted with the paddle attachment (or in a large bowl using an electric hand mixer), beat together the butter, sugar, and hazelnut paste on medium speed, stopping occasionally to scrape down the sides of the bowl, until completely combined, 5 to 7 minutes.

3. With the mixer still running on medium, add the eggs one at a time, waiting until each egg is incorporated before adding the next. Add the vanilla extract.

4. Remove the bowl from the mixer. Using a rubber spatula, fold in the flour, salt, and baking powder.

5. Divide the batter evenly between the prepared pans.

6. Bake until a toothpick inserted in the center of a cake comes out clean or with a few moist crumbs clinging to it, 25 to 30 minutes.

7. Transfer the cakes to a rack to cool in the pans for about 30 minutes. To invert, run a knife or thin metal spatula around the edge of one cake to help loosen it. Invert the cake onto a plate. Remove the cake pan. Place a cake plate on top of the cake, and invert it again so the cake plate is on the bottom. Repeat for the other cake.

8. Let the cakes cool completely before filling, frosting, or storing. Once cool, the unfrosted cakes can be wrapped in plastic wrap and refrigerated for up to 2 days.

Vanilla Swiss Meringue Buttercream

SWISS MERINGUE BUTTERCREAM (SMBC) IS THE KING OF BUTTERCREAMS AND MY frosting of choice. It's silky, smooth, and, unlike some other types of buttercream, doesn't leave a greasy or gritty feeling in your mouth. (Because the sugar is dissolved before adding, it won't form clumps and create an unpleasant texture.) SMBC is a great choice for filling decorated and stacked cakes because it's creamy and delicious, yet it's very stable and holds its shape. SMBC also retains its color well in warmer weather, as opposed to American-style buttercream, which can start to yellow. Finally, this buttercream pipes beautifully and works well as a base when you're adding fondant decorations onto cakes.

MAKES ABOUT 5 CUPS

1 cup granulated sugar

$^1/_2$ cup large egg whites (from about 4 large eggs) or $^1/_2$ cup of pasteurized egg whites

$^1/_4$ tsp. kosher salt

1 pound (4 sticks) cold unsalted butter, cut into small cubes

1 Tbs. pure vanilla extract

Vanilla Chiffon Cake with Blackberry Cabernet Buttercream

NOTE: *You may substitute pasteurized egg whites for raw egg whites. If you do, warm them in the microwave for a few seconds before using them. The meringue will not get as fluffy, but it doesn't have a noticeable effect on the final product.*

1. In a heatproof bowl large enough to fit on top of your saucepan, whisk together the sugar, egg whites, and salt.

2. In a 2-quart saucepan, bring 4 cups of water to a simmer over medium-high heat. Set the bowl over the simmering water (don't let the bowl touch the water) and heat the mixture, whisking occasionally, until the mixture registers 160°F on an instant-read thermometer, 10 to 12 minutes. If using pasteurized egg whites, you don't need to bring the mixture up to 160°F; just heat the mixture until it is warm to the touch.

3. Pour the egg white mixture into the bowl of a stand mixer fitted with the whisk attachment (or a large bowl if using an electric hand mixer). On medium-high speed, beat the egg white mixture until it resembles a white, fluffy cloud, 8 to 10 minutes.

4. Lower the mixer speed to medium low and add the butter, a few cubes at a time. The mixture may begin to appear curdled, but this is okay; keep the mixer running until the buttercream

VARIATIONS

Once you've mastered the basic technique for making SMBC, the variations are endless. Below you'll find a few of my favorites, including toffee, wildflower honey, blackberry cabernet, and, of course, chocolate.

TOFFEE BUTTERCREAM

Line a rimmed baking sheet with foil and spray the foil evenly with cooking spray. Combine 2 cups granulated sugar, 8 ounces (2 sticks) cubed, unsalted butter, and $1^1/_2$ tsp. kosher salt in a heavy-duty 4-quart saucepan. Cook over medium heat until golden brown and bubbling, 8 to 10 minutes. Pour the mixture onto the prepared pan, spread it out with a heatproof spatula, and let it cool completely, until the toffee is hard and cool to the touch, at least 1 hour. Then turn the toffee out onto a cutting board and chop it into small pieces with a chef's knife. Add $1/_2$ cup of chopped toffee to every 2 cups of the Vanilla SMBC. Store the remaining toffee in an airtight container at room temperature for up to 2 weeks.

WILDFLOWER HONEY BUTTERCREAM

Substitute $1/_2$ cup of high-quality wildflower honey for $1/_2$ cup of the granulated sugar in the Vanilla SMBC recipe.

BLACKBERRY-CABERNET BUTTERCREAM

Combine 2 cups cabernet, 1 cup blackberries (smashed with a fork or potato masher), and $1/_4$ cup granulated sugar in a heavy-duty 2-quart saucepan. Cook over medium heat until thickened and reduced by a third, about 20 minutes. The mixture should have the consistency of maple syrup. Strain through a fine sieve and let the syrup cool completely. Stir $1/_4$ cup of the syrup into every 2 cups of Vanilla SMBC. Refrigerate the remaining syrup in an airtight container for up to a week, or freeze it for up to 3 months.

CHOCOLATE BUTTERCREAM

Melt $1/_2$ cup chopped 60% dark chocolate in a microwave-safe bowl on high for 45-second intervals, stirring between each interval, until melted. Set the chocolate aside, stirring occasionally, until cool to the touch, about 20 minutes. Fold the chocolate into 2 cups of Vanilla SMBC using a rubber spatula.

---

is smooth, glossy, and white (it will lighten in color during mixing), 10 to 15 minutes.

5. Add the vanilla extract and beat until incorporated.

6. Use the buttercream immediately or refrigerate in an airtight container for up to a week.

7. To bring refrigerated buttercream back to a useable consistency, transfer it back to the mixer fitted with the whisk attachment. Beat on medium speed until the buttercream is fluffy, about 15 minutes. The mixture may appear curdled before it comes back together.

Chocolate Ganache

WHEN I FIRST BECAME A PASTRY CHEF, CHOCOLATE GANACHE WAS ONE OF THOSE THINGS that completely blew my mind. Where had this magical, three-ingredient wonder been all my life? And why didn't everyone know about it?

Despite its simplicity, ganache is incredibly versatile, since it's easily used as sauce, filling, or frosting. Chocolate is the star of this show, so use the best quality you can get your hands on. Most supermarkets now have a decent chocolate selection in the candy or baking aisle. Choose wrapped, bar-style chocolate for best results, and avoid chips (they contain an ingredient that helps them keep their shape, so they don't melt well). This recipe also calls for Lyle's Golden Syrup®, a pure sugar cane syrup that's available at most supermarkets and specialty stores. It's worth taking the time to find, since a little goes a long way. The flavor of corn syrup pales in comparison, but will do in a pinch. Both syrups help to give the ganache a glossy sheen when set.

MAKES ABOUT 2 CUPS

3 cups chopped dark chocolate (this recipe works with 50% cocao or higher; I prefer 72% cocao for flavor)

2 Tbs. Lyle's Golden Syrup or light corn syrup

2 cups heavy cream

1. Combine the chocolate and syrup in a medium heatproof bowl.

2. In a 2-quart saucepan, bring the cream to a boil over medium-high heat.

3. Remove from the heat, and pour the cream over the chocolate and syrup.

4. Whisk until the ingredients are completely combined and the chocolate is melted. If the mixture begins to cool before the chocolate has melted, set the bowl over a saucepan of simmering water (don't let the bowl touch the water) and gently warm while whisking until combined.

5. At this point, the ganache is perfect for serving as a sauce or for pouring over a chilled, crumb-coated cake as a frosting. To use it as a filling, let the ganache set until it is cool to the touch but still pourable, about 30 minutes.

6. Refrigerate leftover ganache in a plastic container. To reheat, microwave it for short intervals (5 to 20 seconds at a time), stirring in between. If you accidentally overheat the ganache and it "breaks" (the fats and solids separate), add a small amount of very cold heavy cream and whisk until your ganache comes back together.

VARIATIONS

The silky smoothness of ganache relies on a fine balance of fats and solids. Dark, milk, and white chocolates all have different ratios of each. Because of this, you can't simply substitute one chocolate for another in any ganache recipe. The percentage numbers on chocolate tell you what percentage of the chocolate is made up of cocoa solids. Dark chocolate has a percentage of 35% or higher. Milk chocolate has a much lower percentage of solids, and white chocolate has none. Milk and white chocolates still work beautifully in ganache recipes—the method is the same—but the heavy cream must be adjusted so that you don't end up with a soupy mess.

MILK CHOCOLATE GANACHE
Use 1¼ cups heavy cream.

WHITE CHOCOLATE GANACHE
Use 1 cup heavy cream.

Cream Cheese Frosting

I LOVE CREAM CHEESE FROSTING—I'M PRETTY SURE I COULD EAT IT ON JUST ABOUT anything. In my opinion, it makes for the best cupcake frosting. It also works well as a cake filling. Even though this is a very simple recipe, the temperature of the ingredients and the order in which you add them is key. Many recipes call for beating the butter and cream cheese at the same time, but this makes the frosting too soft. Beating the butter first and then adding the cream cheese results in a fluffier frosting. It also makes the frosting much more stable and easier to pipe. This frosting works well with rustic or piped pearl finishes, but it's too soft for rosettes or for piping with a star tip. If you use it to fill a cake, be sure to pipe a dam of buttercream around the edges of your layer first so that it doesn't cause bulges in your cake design (see p. 15).

MAKES ABOUT 5 CUPS

1 pound (4 sticks) cold unsalted butter

1 pound cream cheese, at room temperature

One 2-pound bag (about 7 cups) confectioners' sugar

1 Tbs. pure vanilla extract

1. In the bowl of a stand mixer fitted with the paddle attachment (or in a large bowl if using an electric hand mixer), beat the butter on medium-high speed until it's completely smooth and has no lumps, stopping occasionally to scrape down the sides of the bowl with a rubber spatula, 5 to 7 minutes.

2. Add the cream cheese and continue to beat on medium speed until just combined and the mixture is uniform, 2 to 4 minutes.

3. On low speed, add the confectioners' sugar, 1 cup at a time, and beat until completely incorporated.

4. Add the vanilla extract and beat until just combined.

5. Use immediately or refrigerate the frosting in an airtight container for up to a week. Press a piece of plastic wrap against the surface of the frosting before putting the lid on; this helps to keep the frosting from picking up any flavors from the fridge. To bring refrigerated frosting back to a useable consistency, put it in the bowl of a stand mixer fitted with the paddle attachment (or in a large bowl if using an electric hand mixer) and beat on medium until smooth enough to spread or pipe.

Lemon Curd

LEMON IS ONE OF THOSE LOVE/HATE FLAVORS—YOU EITHER ADORE IT OR YOU DON'T. SO whenever I use it, I like for it to pack a punch, since anyone going for the lemon cake is looking for that puckery-tart taste. Lemon curd should be smooth and creamy in texture. It's a softer filling, so be sure to pipe a buttercream dam around the outer edge of your cake layer before filling (see p. 15). Also, make sure to chill it completely before using; if you pour hot curd into a cake layer, it'll melt the other frostings and fillings and will soak through the cake.

MAKES ABOUT 2 CUPS

2/3 cup granulated sugar

4 large egg yolks

3 large eggs

3/4 cup fresh lemon juice (from 4 to 5 lemons)

2 ounces (1/2 stick) cold unsalted butter, cubed

1/2 tsp. pure vanilla extract

Pinch kosher salt

1. In a medium heatproof bowl, whisk together the sugar, egg yolks, eggs, and lemon juice. (Be sure to use a bowl large enough to sit on the top of your saucepan).

2. In a 2-quart saucepan, bring 4 cups of water to a simmer over medium-high heat. Set the bowl over the simmering water (don't let the bowl touch the water) and heat the mixture, whisking constantly, until thickened (the mixture should have the texture of mayonnaise), about 10 minutes.

3. Remove from the heat and whisk in the butter, vanilla extract, and salt until completely combined.

4. Pour the lemon curd into a plastic or glass container, press plastic wrap on the surface of the curd so a skin doesn't form, and refrigerate until completely chilled, at least 2 hours and up to overnight, before using. The lemon curd will keep, refrigerated, for 2 to 3 days.

Blueberry-Lemon Chiffon Cake with Vanilla SMBC and Lemon Curd

VARIATION

LIME CURD
Substitute 1/2 cup of fresh lime juice (from about 4 limes) for 1/2 cup of the lemon juice.

Pastry Cream

PASTRY CREAM IS A SMOOTH, CUSTARD-LIKE FILLING THAT PAIRS WELL WITH ANYTHING from chocolate to fruity flavors. If you're making a cake with multiple layers, try alternating the pastry cream with other buttercreams or jam. Pastry cream is a softer filling, so pipe a buttercream dam before filling your cake (see p. 15).

MAKES ABOUT 2 CUPS

6 large egg yolks
²/₃ cup granulated sugar
3 Tbs. cornstarch
Pinch kosher salt
2 cups whole milk
1 Tbs. cold unsalted butter
1 Tbs. pure vanilla extract

1. In a large heatproof bowl, whisk together the egg yolks, sugar, cornstarch, and salt.

2. Pour the milk into a heavy-duty, 2-quart saucepan and bring to a boil over medium-high heat. Immediately remove from the heat. Add about 1 cup of the hot milk to the egg mixture and whisk vigorously to combine; this is called "tempering" the mixture, so that the eggs don't scramble in the remaining hot milk. Once tempered, pour the egg mixture into the hot milk. Whisk to combine and return the saucepan to medium-low heat.

3. Continue to cook, stirring constantly with a heatproof spatula or wooden spoon, until thickened (the mixture should have the texture of mayonnaise), 5 to 7 minutes. When you move the spoon through the custard, an open channel should form and quickly close behind it.

4. Remove the custard from the heat and strain it through a fine strainer into a medium bowl. (This will remove any small egg curds that may have formed.)

5. Whisk in the butter and vanilla extract.

6. Press plastic wrap on the surface of the pastry cream so a skin doesn't form, and refrigerate until completely chilled, at least 1 hour and up to overnight, before using. The pastry cream will keep, refrigerated, for 2 to 3 days.

Ginger Chiffon Cake with Pastry Cream and Raspberry Jam Filling

Peanut Butter Frosting

EVEN A FANCY-CAKE PERSON LIKE ME ENJOYS A GOOD OLD-FASHIONED STICKY-SWEET frosting from time to time, and this one doesn't disappoint. Its salty sweetness pairs well with every cake from rich devil's food to classic vanilla chiffon. Layer it on with tart raspberry jam for a sophisticated take on PB&J, or pair it with silky chocolate ganache for a homespun candy bar flavor. This frosting is terrific as a filling, can double as a finisher, and works great with all of the buttercream piping techniques listed in the front of this book. Use any brand of peanut butter you like. For a crunchier texture, substitute natural peanut butter.

MAKES 2 CUPS

8 ounces (2 sticks) unsalted butter, at room temperature

1 cup smooth peanut butter

$1/4$ tsp. kosher salt

1 tsp. pure vanilla extract

3 cups confectioners' sugar

$1/4$ cup whole milk (more or less, depending on how thick you want it to be)

1. In the bowl of a stand mixer fitted with the paddle attachment (or in a large bowl using an electric hand mixer), beat together the butter and the peanut butter on medium speed until well-combined, stopping occasionally to scrape down the sides of the bowl with a rubber spatula. (This ensures that your frosting will be smooth, creamy, and lump-free.)

2. Turn off the mixer and add the salt and vanilla extract. Mix on low speed just until combined, about 1 minute.

3. With the mixer still on low speed, slowly add the confectioners' sugar about $1/4$ cup at a time, until just combined, stopping occasionally to scrape down the sides of the bowl.

4. Keep the mixer on low speed and slowly add the milk until the frosting reaches the desired consistency. For a thicker frosting, add less; for a thinner frosting, add more. (Thicker frosting will work better for piping, while a thinner frosting will spread more easily as a cake filling.)

5. Use immediately, or refrigerate the frosting in an airtight container for up to a week. Bring refrigerated frosting back to a useable consistency by beating it on medium speed in the bowl of a stand mixer fitted with the paddle attachment (or in a large bowl using a hand mixer) until soft and fluffy again.

Salted Caramel

SALTY, SWEET, AND ABSOLUTELY DELICIOUS, THIS CARAMEL CAN BE USED AS A SAUCE when warmed and as a terrific cake filling when chilled. It can be very rich, so if you're filling multiple cake layers, try alternating it with a complementary flavor. (I like using it on the Hazelnut Cake on p. 197, along with Toffee Buttercream on p. 199. Together, the flavors remind me of a candy bar.) You can also make salted caramel buttercream by folding 1/2 cup of room temperature caramel into one batch of Vanilla Swiss Meringue Buttercream (see p. 198).

MAKES 4 CUPS

3 cups granulated sugar

1 1/2 cups heavy cream

1 Tbs. kosher salt or sea salt

1 Tbs. fresh orange juice

1 tsp. pure vanilla extract

6 ounces (1 1/2 sticks) cold unsalted butter, cut into cubes

1. Combine the sugar and 1 cup of water in a heavy-duty, 4-quart saucepan. Cook over medium-high heat until dark amber in color, about 10 minutes. Don't stir the caramel, or you can cause sugar crystals to form. If sugar crystals begin to form around the edges of the caramel, use a pastry brush to brush the sides of the pan with water. If the caramel begins to darken more in one spot than another, gently swirl the pan to move the caramel around.

2. Remove from the heat and let the caramel stop bubbling completely. Whisk in the heavy cream. Be very careful—the cream can sputter when added to the caramel.

3. Whisk in the salt, orange juice, and vanilla extract.

4. Whisk in the butter.

5. To use the caramel right away as a sauce, spoon it onto your dessert or pour it into a plastic squeeze bottle. If using as a filling, pour the caramel into a heat-safe container and refrigerate for at least 3 hours. The caramel can be refrigerated for up to a week.

6. To fill a cake with the caramel, first pipe a buttercream dam around the edges of your cake according to the instructions on p. 15. Spread the chilled caramel inside the buttercream dam. Do not use hot caramel as a filling, since it will soak into the cake and melt the buttercream.

Royal Icing

UNLIKE BUTTERCREAM, WHICH STAYS SOFT, ROYAL ICING WILL DRY OUT COMPLETELY when exposed to air. This makes it a great tool for attaching fondant decorations to a cake. It also works well for piping decorations like dots and lines.

MAKES ABOUT 3 CUPS

3/4 cup pasteurized egg whites (available in a carton in the egg section of the supermarket)

1 tsp. pure vanilla extract, any other flavored extract, or lemon juice

4 cups confectioners' sugar

1. In a stand mixer fitted with the whisk attachment (or in a large bowl using an electric hand mixer), beat the egg whites on medium high until frothy, 4 to 5 minutes.

2. Add the vanilla extract or other flavoring and beat until combined. With the mixer on low, add the confectioners' sugar about 1 cup at a time until combined.

3. Turn the mixer speed to high and beat until the icing has thickened and forms stiff peaks, 8 to 10 minutes.

4. At this point, the icing will be stiff enough for piping dots or lines. This is also the consistency you'll want if using the icing between cake tiers or to attach decorations.

5. For a thinner icing, add a tablespoon of water at a time until you reach the desired consistency.

6. Store royal icing in an airtight container and refrigerate for up to 2 days. Before putting the lid on the container, press plastic wrap against the surface of the icing; this helps to keep it from drying out. To bring refrigerated icing back to a useable consistency, stir with a spoon until smooth.

Marshmallow Fondant

VERY TASTY AND EASY TO WORK WITH, FONDANT CAN BE MADE AT HOME WITH JUST A FEW simple ingredients. This is a great recipe to try if you can't find good-quality fondant in your area, or if you're in a pinch and need some for a last-minute cake. Like store-bought fondant, this version needs to be stored tightly wrapped in plastic wrap. You can color homemade fondant using gel food colors, if you like; you can also add flavor with clear extracts by substituting them for the vanilla.

A note about the marshmallows: Many decorators use mini marshmallows for homemade fondant, but regular marshmallows work too. The mini marshmallows are just a little easier to portion and work with, but their flavor and texture are essentially the same as the large ones. Mini marshmallows may be easier to use if you're cutting the recipe in half to make a smaller batch.

MAKES JUST OVER 2 POUNDS

One 16-ounce package marshmallows (mini or regular)

2 tsp. pure vanilla extract or any flavored extract

One 2-pound bag (about 7 cups) confectioners' sugar, sifted

1/4 cup vegetable shortening

Gel food color (optional)

1. Put the marshmallows in a large microwave-safe bowl and microwave on high until melted, 1 minute.

2. Stir the marshmallows with a rubber spatula. If some lumps remain, continue to microwave for about 30 seconds. Stir the marshmallows again until smooth and completely melted.

3. Add 3 tablespoons of water and the extract to the marshmallows and stir to combine.

4. Add the confectioners' sugar to the marshmallow mixture about 1 cup at a time, stirring the mixture to combine and continuing to add the sugar until the mixture is difficult to stir.

5. With your hands, rub some of the vegetable shortening onto your work surface. (Having the shortening on your hands will also make the kneading process a little easier.) The amount of shortening you end up using will depend on the humidity where you're working. Knead in more shortening if the mixture appears dry.

6. Scrape the marshmallow mixture onto the greased work surface and continue kneading in the sugar until the mixture is smooth. (Whether you use all of the sugar will depend on the humidity. If it's more humid, you'll need more sugar.)

7. If using, add gel food color to the fondant according to the directions on p. 25. Then wrap the fondant tightly in plastic wrap and store in a zip-top bag at room temperature. Make note of the expiration date on the bag of marshmallows and use the fondant before then.

8. Stored fondant may become tough over time. To bring it back to a useable consistency, remove the plastic wrap and knead the fondant with a little bit of vegetable shortening until smooth. If the fondant is too dry or tough to knead, microwave it for 3 to 5 seconds to make it pliable again.

Transporting a Cake

AFTER BAKING, FILLING, FINISHING, AND DECORATING A CAKE, YOU MAY HAVE TO MOVE it to the event for which it was made. It's scary, I know—I still have a little superstitious routine that I do before moving more intricate cakes. I talk myself up, like a baseball player would, to convince myself I can do it. Confidence is key, but proper planning is even more important.

There are two schools of thought when it comes to moving a cake. The first is the more-you-see method. Meaning, the more you see of the cake while moving it, the less likely you are to do anything bad to it. Placing the cake in the back of a vehicle with a flat open space (like an SUV), can be a quick and easy way to move it—you'll just need a nonskid mat on which to place the cake. You can purchase one made for transporting cakes at a cake supply store, or you can pick up a thin nonskid bath mat at a store that sells home goods. Remember to take it easy when driving around corners, and make sure there aren't any objects in the back of the car that could bump the cake. I've seen many cakes make it safely to their destination this way.

The second method is to box the cake. If you have a long distance to travel or are nervous about leaving the cake exposed in your vehicle, this is the way to go. Lowering a tiered cake into a box and then lifting it back out would be very difficult. It's easier to cut a flap into the side of a box so you can slide the cake in and out. To make the box, start with a heavy-duty cardboard box (like a moving box) that is taller than the cake. (Most moving supply stores carry boxes this large. If your cake is larger than 18 inches high, you should probably box it in smaller segments and stack the cake on-site.) The box should be as wide as the cake board; you want the cake board to fit up against the sides. This helps to keep the cake board from sliding around. If you can only find boxes wider than the cake board, you can fill the gap with Styrofoam.

To prepare the box, assemble it and tape it shut on all sides with packing tape. Yes, the box is empty, but you will be cutting into it to create a pull-down door through which you can slide the cake. To make the door, place the box vertically on a work surface. Carefully cut up the left side of the box, just inside its edge. Continue cutting across the top side of the box, just below the top edge, and then cut down the right side, just inside the edge. Leave the bottom edge intact. Pull down the flap you just created, and slide the cake into the box. Lift up the flap and seal it with packing tape.

Getting the cake there is only half the battle. Once at the party location, it's important to know what kind of cake obstacle course awaits you when getting from the car to the cake table. If you're headed to a restaurant or other venue, call ahead and let them know you'll be bringing in a cake. Ask if there's anything important you should know about, like flights of stairs, vertical driveways, or the dog that sits by the front door. When you get to the location, always go in first without the cake so you can scout where you're headed and make a plan.

If your cake is more than three tiers, I suggest assembling it on-site. If you have very delicate decorations like gum paste flowers or bows, it might be better to carry them in separately and apply them to the cake where it will be presented. After setting up the cake, make sure you tell someone at the venue before you leave. This is important, because you don't want anyone moving your cake or touching it once you've gone.

How Much Is Enough?

THE FOLLOWING AMOUNTS OF FONDANT AND BUTTERCREAM ARE FOR CAKES THAT are about 5 inches high. The amounts of fondant here are measured using a scale, but you can eyeball the amount needed based on the size of your fondant container. Keep in mind that you might actually need a little less or a little more, depending on how comfortable you are working with fondant or buttercream. If you're just starting out, my advice is to always have a little more on hand than you need. The buttercream amounts are for a smooth finish. Piped or layered finishes will require more.

CAKE SIZE	FONDANT	BUTTERCREAM
6-inch round	$1\frac{1}{2}$ pounds	3 cups
8-inch round	2 pounds	5 cups
10-inch round	$2\frac{1}{2}$ pounds	8 cups
12-inch round	$3\frac{1}{2}$ pounds	10 cups
14-inch round	$4\frac{1}{2}$ pounds	12 cups
6-inch square	2 pounds	4 cups
8-inch square	$2\frac{1}{2}$ pounds	6 cups
10-inch square	$3\frac{1}{2}$ pounds	9 cups
12-inch square	$4\frac{1}{2}$ pounds	11 cups
14-inch square	5 pounds	13 cups

Metric Equivalents

LIQUID/DRY MEASURES	
U.S.	**METRIC**
¼ teaspoon	1.25 milliliters
½ teaspoon	2.5 milliliters
1 teaspoon	5 milliliters
1 tablespoon (3 teaspoons)	15 milliliters
1 fluid ounce (2 tablespoons)	30 milliliters
¼ cup	60 milliliters
⅓ cup	80 milliliters
½ cup	120 milliliters
1 cup	240 milliliters
1 pint (2 cups)	480 milliliters
1 quart (4 cups; 32 ounces)	960 milliliters
1 gallon (4 quarts)	3.84 liters
1 ounce (by weight)	28 grams
1 pound	454 grams
2.2 pounds	1 kilogram

OVEN TEMPERATURES		
°F	**GAS MARK**	**°C**
250	½	120
275	1	140
300	2	150
325	3	165
350	4	180
375	5	190
400	6	200
425	7	220
450	8	230
475	9	240
500	10	260
550	Broil	290

Resources

BAKEWARE, KITCHEN EQUIPMENT
Amazon
Amazon.com

Ebay (hard to find or discontinued pans and tools)
www.ebay.com

J. B. Prince Company
www.jbprince.com

Kerkes Bakery & Restaurant Equipment
www.kerekesequip.com

King Arthur Flour
www.kingarthurflour.com

Sur La Table
www.surlatable.com

The Webstaurant Store
www.webstaurantstore.com

Williams-Sonoma
www.williams-sonoma.com

DECORATING TOOLS
Beryl's Cake Decorating Supplies
www.beryls.com

CalJava
www.caljavaonline.com

Copper Gifts
www.coppergifts.com

Country Kitchen SweetArt, Inc.
www.countrykitchenusa.com

Decorate The Cake
www.decoratethecake.com

Etsy
www.etsy.com

Fondarific
www.fondarific.com

Global Sugar Art
www.globalsugarart.com

Make Your Own Molds
www.makeyourownmolds.com

NY Cake
www.nycake.com

Pfeil & Holing
www.cakedeco.com

Satin Ice
www.satinice.com

Sugar Delites
www.jenniferdontz.com

Sugar Wand Enterprises
www.cakesbydesign.cc

Sugarcraft
www.sugarcraft.com

Sunflower Sugar Art
www.sunflowersugarart.com

Wilton Industries
www.wilton.com

X-ACTO
www.xacto.com

OTHER SUPPLIES
Guildcraft Furniture
www.guildcraftfurniture.com/cake-dummies

Jo-Ann
www.joann.com

Michael's Craft Stores
www.michaels.com

Paper Mart
www.papermart.com

Target
www.target.com

Trader Joe's
www.traderjoes.com

Walmart
www.walmart.com

CAKE DECORATING INFORMATION
Cake Central®
www.cakecentral.com

Cakes Decor
www.cakesdecor.com

Edible Artists Network
www.edibleartistsnetwork.com

International Cake Exploration Societé
www.ices.org

Index

Numbers in **bold** indicate pages with illustrations